THE OFFICIAL
TOUR DE FRANCE
BIKE
MAINTENANCE
BOOK

This book is available in quantity at special
discounts for your group or organization. For
further information, contact:
Triumph Books LLC
814 North Franklin Street
Chicago, Illinois 60610
(312) 337-0747
www.triumphbooks.com

ISBN 978-1-62937-692-9

Editorial Director: Martin Corteel
Project Editor: Ross Hamilton
Design Manager: Luke Griffin
Designers: James Pople and Harj Ghundale
Picture Research: Paul Langan
Production: Rachel Burgess

Printed in Dubai

Author's acknowledgements
The author would like to thank mechanics
Geoff Brown, Ryan Bonser and Rohan Dubash
(www.doctord.co.uk) for their help and advice.

THE OFFICIAL
TOUR DE FRANCE
BIKE
MAINTENANCE
BOOK

HOW TO PREP YOUR BIKE LIKE THE PROS

LUKE EDWARDES-EVANS

30 YEARS
TRIUMPH
BOOKS

CONTENTS

Every cyclist dreams of riding the Tour de France. Since the first edition in 1903, the epic three-week race quickly earned a reputation as the most prestigious and gruelling annual challenge for the world's top cyclists.

Only the great champions were capable of winning the Tour and a glance at the roll of honour confirms that, with the names of Eddie Merckx, Fausto Coppi, Bernard Hinault, Miguel Indurain and Chris Froome jumping out as just some of the legends who have won the Tour multiple times. To win a single stage of the race is also a career highlight for any professional cyclist. Such is the prestige of a Tour win it can guarantee a rider's contract for the following year and beyond.

Taking place in the heart of summer the Tour de France is a three-week Grand Tour consisting of 21 consecutive days of racing and roughly 3,500km with only two rest days at the beginning of the second and third weeks. Every year the Tour route is different, with a mixture of road stages and time trials designed to test the all-round abilities of the peloton. When the route is announced in the autumn the year before, riders and fans pore over stages, assessing their length, the amount of hills and mountains, and cobbles and time trials, to see which champion will be best suited to the next edition.

There are other factors which affect the outcome of the Tour. Often the weather in July can be extremely hot, or very wet and sometimes cold especially in the Alps and Pyrenees. If the race starts outside of France, which the Grand Depart has done

on many occasions, unfamiliar roads can be made worse in bad weather and high-speed crashes in the bunch are an unfortunate consequence of first week nerves.

There are 22 teams in the modern Tour, with eight riders on each making a total peloton at the start of 176 riders. Behind every team has a support crew, all dedicated to ensuring their eight riders are in the best possible shape for the three-week race. From sports directors who drive the cars behind the race and issue commands to the riders on their race radios, to the team chef who prepares super-healthy breakfast and dinners, only the best personnel make it to the Tour.

And the same goes for the heroes and subjects of this book: the four or so mechanics on each team dedicated to maintaining all the team bikes in race winning condition. Team mechanics are, like the cyclists who ride the Tour, at the very top of their profession. A cyclist dreams of riding the Tour. A bicycle mechanic dreams of becoming one of the elite cadre who make it to the Tour.

In the Official Tour de France Bike Maintenance book we go behind the barriers of the team mechanic's trucks and team buses at the Tour starts and finishes and marvel at the many jobs and skills of the pro Tour mechanic. Speed, efficiency and perfectionism are the Tour mechanic's stock in trade and they carry out their duties with unfailing good humour. With advice, tips and step-by-step guides the home bicycle mechanic can prepare their bike to Tour de France standards. You may not get to ride the Tour but with the *Official Tour de France Maintenance Book* you can feel like one!

▶ **A ride in the Tour is the ultimate test for cyclists and their mechanics.**

A team travels to the Tour with all their bikes and accessories in one, very valuable, truck.

From the high mountains to the brutal cobbles and high-speed time trials, there is a Tour bike for every discipline.

CHAPTER 1:

TOUR BIKES

Modern road racing bikes are light, fast and they look sensational. Under the carbon fibre skin they are more robust and reliable than the steel and aluminium bikes of old. One machine can do it all, but the Tour de France is so competitive that riders use different machines for each type of stage. When every second counts, the best machine suited to the conditions could be the bike that makes the difference between winning and losing.

Flat or rolling stages make up the majority of kilometres covered by the Tour peloton. Stages of over 200 kilometres (124 miles) can take five hours or more and the bunch can hit speeds in excess of 70kph (43mph) in the build-up and execution of a field sprint. Roads can vary from expansive and smooth to cramped and twisty, with riders fighting for advantageous positions near the front, or nervously confined in the low-drag centre of the bunch.

In the first week of the Tour, every team is eager either to score a stage win or to protect its leading riders for later in the race. There is a lot of stress as the risk takers battle for stage wins, while more cautious squads mass near to the front where they hope to avoid a big pile-up. In these situations the requirement is for a bike with impeccable handling but also a degree of comfort. Brakes with plenty of feel and consistency are essential, too.

Aerodynamics determines the looks, with frames developed in wind tunnels, cables hidden from sight and wheels designed to scythe through the air. On a road bike these bladed or aerofoil-shaped parts must conform to specifications laid down by the world governing body – the Union Cycliste Internationale (UCI) – as well as perform safely and predictably in windy conditions. A rider who selects the wrong type of aero wheel might regret his decision if strong crosswinds blow up later in the stage.

AERO FRAMESET

Wind tunnel research is the reason modern road race frames are composed of sleek aerofoil spars designed to cut through the air with minimal drag. Regulations ensure that the depth of the spars or tubes cannot exceed a ratio of roughly three times its width. In profile, an aero road frame still resembles the traditional diamond frame made from skinny steel tubes going back more than a century.

FORK

Disc brake-enabled forks are designed to fit as snugly as possible under the head tube of the frame and have threaded inserts on one side for a direct-mount disc caliper. A traditional fork has open dropouts for the wheel but a modern disc brake fork can have closed ends with one side threaded, into which a hollow thru-axle is screwed. This method of wheel attachment resists twisting forces from the disc brake and guarantees it cannot move in the fork end. It can also make fast wheel changes a real challenge for a stressed-out mechanic.

INTEGRATED PARTS

From the cockpit, where the stem and bars join the head tube, back to the end of the chainstays where an electronic cable

▶ Disc brakes are increasingly a feature on bikes used for flat and sprint stages of the Tour.

is barely visible as it plugs into the rear derailleur, integrated parts are everywhere. Designed specifically for each type of frame, the stem and bars are a flush fit with the top of the head tube, and often include mounts for computers and hidden guides for cables and wires. There's an aerodynamic advantage and an aesthetic one too, helped significantly by the adoption of electronic gears operated either via virtually maintenance-free cables, or wirelessly.

WHEELS

It may not look like it but a modern road race wheel is basically the same combination of hub, spokes and rim that it has always been. Carbon fibre has replaced the alloy of the hub and rim, and sometimes the steel or alloy of the spokes, too. But the wheel still relies on individually tensioned spokes to give strength to the rim and ensure it remains in true. A wheel for road racing can feature a shallower rim designed for a more forgiving ride, which is less susceptible to crosswinds. The adoption of disc brakes also allows for a rim shaped purely for aerodynamics and low weight, usefully reducing gyroscopic inertia. The hub must incorporate a disc mount that adds some weight and the wheel must also be capable of resisting the extra twisting forces of an offset disc brake.

▼ A cutting-edge flat road stage bike with an aerodynamic frame and components – and barely a cable or wire in sight.

TOUR TIP

Tyres on road bikes are now typically 25c in size compared to 23c just a few years ago, running at lower pressures offering a more comfortable ride with no loss in rolling resistance.

COBBLED OR UNMADE ROAD STAGE BIKE

A single stage with cobbled sections or even part of a stage with a section on unmade roads can significantly affect the outcome of the three-week Tour de France. Tour riders with aspirations for the general classifications are rarely suited to the rough and tumble of the infamous one-day classic races on the cobbled roads and climbs of Belgium and northern France. In Italy, the Strade Bianche race has become one of the hardest one-day races on the calendar and features many kilometres on treacherous unmade roads in Tuscany.

These events have led to the development of bikes suited to bumpy roads where crashes and punctures can wreck a rider's day. As the saying goes: you may not win the Tour after a day on the cobbles, but you can certainly lose it. Such is the prestige of the modern Tour that teams are prepared to equip competitors with bikes just for one stage on the cobbles if it improves the chances of their leading riders finishing safely, and without losing crucial seconds.

A bike equipped to conquer the cobbles must achieve two things above all others: resist punctures and provide stable handling over rough terrain. Tyre and wheel choice determines the former, while frame design and tyre pressures the latter. Both are connected, as a bike that is easier to control on cobbles will allow the rider to deftly avoid hard edges and gravel.

▼ A tour bike for a cobbled stage with oversize road tyres, a more forgiving frame and disc brakes allowing plenty of clearance for the tyres.

TYRES

Fatter and less inflated than a normal road tyre, tyre choice and pressure is the most important thing to get right on a bike for racing over cobbles. A standard road tyre would be 23mm to 25mm (1in) diameter whereas for cobbles the diameter can be 27mm to 30mm (1¼in). The extra volume provided by a fatter tyre allows for lower tyre pressures, which help to absorb patter and bigger hits from potholes and raised stones. These tyres, known as tubulars or sew-ups, resemble a single tube and must be glued to the rim. Tubular tyres are favoured by professional riders as they are less prone to pinch or snake-bite punctures when the tyre is pushed back to the rim. They can also be ridden for longer when they are flat, minimising the distance to chase back to the bunch after a wheel change.

ALUMINIUM PARTS

Crashes are inevitable when 176 furiously pedalling cyclists funnel down a farm track laid with jagged cobblestones. Carbon fibre parts can withstand a pounding but do not react well to impacts. They crack and shatter dangerously. For a cobbles bike the team mechanics will swap out carbon bars and stems and replace them with aluminium versions which are more likely to bend and allow a rider to continue. Carbon bottle cages can also be changed for aluminium ones with grip tape to prevent the bottle flying out.

FRAMESET

These are carbon fibre but with thicker sections for strength and sometimes incorporate elements of the brand's flagship

◀ Before a cobbled stage, grip tape is applied to bottle cages to prevent bottles bouncing out.

customer endurance model intended for all-day rides in comfort. This would normally involve a more relaxed geometry and handling tuned for stability. More radical designs incorporate suspension, either with integrated dampers or with tuned carbon tubes and pivots, or a more traditional mini shock unit. Not every rider favours a suspension bike for the cobbles. Some will just ask for another layer of bar tape to protect their hands from the constant jarring.

COMPONENTS

Mechanics will add satellite shifters to the centre or ends of the bars, allowing the rider to change gear without moving their hands around the bars. Normally, only sprinters request satellite shifters but on the cobbles one slip of the hand over a bump could result in a spill. They may even add an additional small brake lever in the centre of the bars. Gears will also be changed as there are rarely hills to negotiate on cobbled road stages. The cassette may have a 25-tooth bottom gear with a bigger inner front ring, 44 or 46T, to allow a wide range of gears for the flat and also enabling the rider to continue riding strongly if the electric front derailleur packs up.

In a typical Tour de France of 2,500km (1,553 miles) there might be roughly 100km (62 miles) of time trialling, in two or three stages. That's four per cent of the total race mileage. A tiny amount, but those kilometres are some of the hardest fought and most decisive in the whole race. These high-speed solo efforts strike fear into the top riders as they know that there is no plan B when a time trial goes wrong.

Time trialling is a high stakes game, which has heated up in recent times as the aerodynamic arms race has forced every top team into the wind tunnel. A modern time trial bike is an arresting sight, with a seat towering above an aerofoil chassis powered by a growling rear disc wheel.

The TT bike is one of cycling's most specialist machines. Its only job is to cleave the air and position the rider in the most extreme aero tuck he can sustain.

A road bike has many aerodynamic features. On a TT (Time Trial) bike they are taken to an extreme with the most obvious difference being the handlebars which bring the rider's elbows together to reduce the frontal area. Wheels can also push the limits with a full carbon fibre rear and three to five-spoke front. A Tour TT bike looks ballistic standing still.

LOW-PROFILE FRAME

Maximum aerodynamic efficiency in a straight line is the sole requirement, which explains a down tube the thickness of a helicopter rotor blade and razor-tipped seat mast. Every tube is either flattened or

▼ A solid rear disc wheel and narrow tri-bar extensions are only permitted in solo and team time trials.

aerofoil-shaped and is designed to either cut through the air or flow it around a component like a brake caliper. Much design input is concentrated on the front end from the forks up to the head tube and fitment of the tri-bars. As much as possible is flush mounted or concealed under a cover.

TRI-BARS

These are custom tuned for each rider to deliver an elbows-in tuck for minimal frontal area. The trend is for a slightly higher elbow rest, moving the upper arms closer to the face but maintaining a flat back. Electronic gear buttons are located on the ends of both bars and also often on the wings, which extend either side of the tri-bars. To operate the skeletal brake levers the rider must move his hands to the wings. Braking is clearly not a priority when travelling in the maximum speed position of a Tour TT bike. The wing hand-holds are only used for starts, climbs and cornering.

BRAKES

In a race where maintaining a high average speed is everything, brakes are a necessary evil. Hiding the brake calipers from the wind is essential but as fairings or aerodynamic covers are not permitted, the brake must either be designed for a flush fit against its mounting point or hidden behind, or even inside, the fork. It's easier to conceal the rear brake behind the seat stays or bottom bracket. Disc brakes are appearing on TT bikes and they will almost certainly evolve into more aerodynamic shapes for this specialist application.

WHEELS

A rear disc wheel is the norm for the majority of time trials. Typically made from two sheets of layered carbon with a carbon or alloy rim, the air flows smoothly over the surface without the churning effect of spokes. Like the rest of the TT bike, it's a very rigid component with zero concessions to comfort. Most Tour time trials take less than one hour to race and are usually on smooth roads. A disc wheel on the front would be too unstable in cross winds so most riders opt for a conventionally spoked front with a deep carbon rim. The spokes are bladed or flat and made from alloy, steel or carbon. Alternatively, a three to five-spoke carbon wheel offers minimal drag but can weigh more and offer less feedback than a spoked front.

TIME TRIAL PARTS

There are some obvious special TT accessories, like the aero bottle that sits behind the down tube and is designed to extend its trailing edge. Less visually aerodynamic are components like the seat and chainrings, which help to position the rider in an aero tuck and give him the higher gears to maintain speeds in excess of 50kph (31mph). The seat with its snub nose is actually a result of regulations designed to ensure the rider does not sit too far forward of the bottom bracket. Measured from the nose, the TT seat can extend the rider's position by a centimetre or so. More power can be generated if the rider is over, or just in front of, the bottom bracket and that allows for the fitment of a bigger chainring.

On long steep climbs like Alpe d'Huez and Mont Ventoux, an ultra-lightweight bike is still favoured over a slightly heavier aero road bike by the specialist climbers and general classification favourites of the Tour de France. Cycling's governing body sets the weight limit for all racing bikes in the Tour at 6.8kg (15lb). That's very light and although it is possible to assemble a rule-breaking stripped-out machine weighing significantly less, the growing adoption of disc brakes and additional components like power cranks have kept the 6.8kg limit relevant.

Increasingly the Tour likes to feature novel climbs with extreme gradients and locations which thrill the crowds and inevitably result in exciting racing. Short mountain stages of 100km (62 miles) or even less are designed to create fast and unpredictable racing and if the climbs are steeper than six per cent there is a small but possibly race wining advantage to a lightweight climbing bike bang on the 6.8kg weight limit than an aero road bike which may be a few hundred grams over it.

In looks, the climber's bike is the most traditional in profile, with a frameset composed mostly of round carbon tubes and often with a round seatpost. With shallow carbon rims and standard spokes the wheels look conventional. As yet there are few disc brake climbing bikes because they still weigh more than standard cable-operated calipers.

▼ **Ultra-light wheels and gram-saving cable operated brakes feature on a pure climbing bike.**

LIGHTWEIGHT FRAMESET

Not that long ago a frame without the fork was considered ultra-light if it weighed less than one kilogram (2¼lb). Today a frame and the fork can be close to the magic one kilogram, but only if it is a non-aero design equipped for stock caliper brakes. An aero frame demands more carbon for complex and deeper tubes or spars and extra material is also required around the mounting points for the hydraulic brake calipers. Without the need for a low drag design the frameset for a climbing stage can revert to a more classic shape, with round carbon tubes of a smaller diameter and a more conventional looking fork.

WHEELS

As with the frame, if the requirement for minimal drag is lower down the list the wheels can be built with the lightest rims available using low profile carbon rims and fitted with lightweight tubular tyres. Keeping the weight down reduces the reciprocating mass in this crucial area and encourages a rapid pick-up when the rider makes stinging accelerations on the steepest inclines. A heavier deep section aero rim will feel sluggish in comparison and can also feel very nervous on descents if it's windy. The only trade-off with a conventional wheel is that a disc brake-equipped version could offer a racing advantage but is not currently light enough to be seriously considered. Once the weight difference is negligible, however, the rim could potentially be made even lighter.

REAR DERAILLEUR

Oversize jockey wheels are a popular optional extra on the pro climbing bike. Intricately machined and very 'rad' looking, they are made from aluminium and come in various anodised colours. A pro bike can look like a top-of-the-range customer machine but few are kitted out with these exotic and expensive oversize jockey wheels. They allow the chain to take a more relaxed route between both wheels and the ceramic bearings are virtually friction-free. All pro bikes benefit from this modification but the climber's psyche can be fragile when the heat is on and they need to know that nothing on the bike is robbing them of precious watts. That could be another reason why the faintest rub from a misaligned disc brake has delayed their appearance on climbing bikes.

COMPONENTS

Aero handlebars have an aerofoil-shaped top section which can add weight and is not as comfortable to hold as a conventional round bar, where a climber will spend much time when pedalling uphill. The carbon seatpost may also be round, as it must be if the seat tube is also round. On a stiff carbon frame a smaller diameter carbon seatpost can be designed to offer a small amount of flex, absorbing low level vibration from the road. A power meter fitted to the chainset adds weight but is an essential rider aid on long climbs. Some climbers will know exactly what their power output should be for each scenario and they will do that by watching the figures displayed on a computer mounted on the stem.

EMERGENCY SPARE BIKE

▲ Mavic's bright yellow bikes and equally eye-catching neutral service car are one of the sights of the Tour.

The Tour de France is the biggest and best organised race in the world. Every team is supported by its own team cars, which drive in a long convoy behind the peloton. On the cars are spare bikes and wheels for every rider. Inside is a mechanic with more spares and wheels. These team cars will service the riders when they puncture or crash and 99 times out of 100 the rider will be back on the road on one of the team's spare bikes or wheels.

But there is always that one time when the team car cannot reach its rider in time and that is when the neutral service car is called into action. On a mountain stage when the bunch has split into multiple groups a Mavic car or scooter with wheels might be the only support vehicles in attendance to some smaller groups. On a cobbled stage with individual riders and groups spread over a wide area the same situation can occur and are made worse when team cars cannot pass even small groups on narrow roads. Mostly it's spare wheels but occasionally a rider will need one of Mavic's bright yellow spare bikes.

It would be impossible on the three or four Mavic service vehicles to have spare bikes assembled to match the proliferation of different systems on modern race bikes. Gone are the days when the Tour peloton rode virtually identical machines. Today there are numerous pedal systems, groupsets, wheels and even brake types. With only room for six bikes on the roof of

each Mavic spare car, all they can do is have a limited range of sizes and pedal systems, allowing a stranded rider to at least engage the pedals on a machine that roughly fits. If all else is failing the mechanic in the back seat can sometimes improvise a fix, because even if the rider finishes well behind the winner, just crossing the line is a victory of sorts in the Tour.

FRAME

This used to be a basic aluminium frame but now is carbon fibre, often an ex-race frame sourced from one of the teams. They come in a range of sizes with twin bottle cages, empty as the rider will normally swap his bottles over. They're painted bright yellow in Mavic colours, as are the cars and scooters. Equipped with a mid-range groupset and with the heavier seatpost fitted the complete spare weighs less than a kilogram more than the lightest Tour road bike.

DROPPER POST

No need for a time consuming and fiddly operation with a hex key to raise or lower the seatpost, which might still be at the wrong height. Dropper posts were designed for mountain bikers who like to raise and lower their saddles while on the move, to lower the centre of gravity and free up space for technical descending. The modified version offers 65mm (2½in) of travel and can be operated with the rider seated, shaving valuable seconds in an emergency. Pulling on a loop while exerting pressure on the seat lowers the post while, much like an office chair, reducing pressure on the saddle allows the post to extend.

PEDALS

A rider can cope with a different saddle and bars. Even if the seat is at the wrong height it can be raised or lowered to approximately match the rider's preferred setting. The gears and brakes might feel alien, too, but it takes a few moments to adapt. If the pedals are not compatible with the rider's shoe plates, however, the shoes will not click in and will just skid off when pressure is applied. This has been an ongoing headache for some time for the neutral service bikes and until recently some of the spare bikes were fitted with old fashioned pedals with toe clips and straps which could at least hold the foot in place and be secured with the ratchet strap. Mavic now equips its spares with one of each of the three most popular pedal systems, ensuring in most cases that the rider can at least engage with the pedals.

COMPONENTS

There is no need for electronic gears on a spare bike. Traditional cable-operated gears work almost as well and there is no battery to go flat either. Mavic's spare bikes are assembled with mid-range groupsets that offer virtually the same level of performance for a negligible trade-off in weight. The same goes for aluminium bars and stem and the conventional caliper brakes. Mavic's proprietary carbon wheels are fitted with Mavic tubular tyres. The wheels are former team items, passed on to Mavic after a season in the peloton.

▲ If a rider is forced to take a Mavic spare bike, you can be sure he has run out of options and his team car is AWOL!

The service course is where the team assembles its bikes for the season, as well as being its administrative headquarters.

CHAPTER 2:

BUILDING A TOUR BIKE

Before the Tour every July, all of the 22 selected teams work long hours to prepare all the bikes and spares for the biggest race of the year. So prestigious is the Tour that many teams will arrive with new bikes, some of them being revealed on the world stage for the first time. Interest in new models and even just the standard race bikes reaches fever pitch in July and the publicity gained from media coverage is immense. All these machines are built and prepared by the team mechanics in the weeks leading up to the Tour.

Located in anonymous units on industrial estates around Europe are warehouses and workshops where the fastest and most exotic bikes it the world are prepared and stored. Welcome to the 'service course' headquarters of the world's top pro cycling teams. There could be one in your home town and you may not know it – keeping a low profile makes sense when you have so much equipment inside, some of it priceless. In fact, during the course of a season it would be hard for a bike fan not to notice colourful team cars, trucks and buses going to and from these locations, such is the year-round 24/7 workload of the modern pro team.

Service course units are typically located on the outskirts of towns, affording easy access to motorways and a nearby airport. Cycling is a sport that is constantly on the move, not just from different race locations in Europe but between continents. Races are more international than ever and so are the personnel employed – riders and staff must be able to fly easily and drive in and out of the service course.

Often the location of the team HQ reflects the core nationality of the team and, with employees drawn from the region as well as riders living locally, the identity and character of the team can remain strongly associated with a country or region. That is still the case with some teams, and is often reflected in their supporters, who can be as fervent and loyal as the fans of a football team. Other teams have become so international in their composition and outlook that their service course location ceases to play to fans that could be drawn from all over the world.

A team HQ is a factory, a warehouse and an office. It combines all the hardware and logistics of the team, with back office jobs which include staff booking all the travel and accommodation. There are rooms set aside for riders and staff to gather for meetings and enough space to park all the team vehicles. During the season staff and riders are coming and going all the time, either travelling to races or returning, with most teams running at least two race programmes.

▶ A spacious and fully equipped workshop in the service course.

▶▶ Bare frames on the right are built up and racked on the left side.

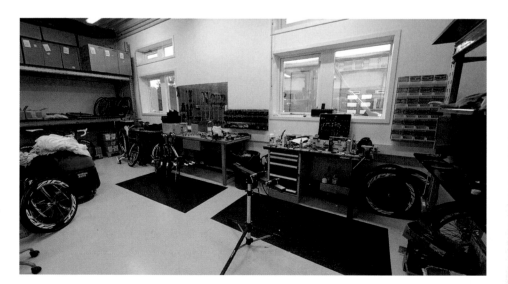

NEW BIKE SEASON

Mechanics may not cross paths for months on end, only coming together as a complete group in the off-season when all the new bikes for the season are assembled. November and December are good months for building up the bikes for the new season, as it gives the mechanics a short break after the final races in October and there is also time for the new frames, groupsets and finishing kits to arrive at the service course. It also means there will be new bikes for the first team training camps which begin in December and January.

Some teams will get all the mechanics together for a week or so of intensive bike building sometime towards the end of the year. This is a good chance for mechanics who may not have seen much of each other during the season to catch up, compare notes and enjoy a few meals together in the local town. It's also an ideal time for any of the team's equipment suppliers and partners to run presentations and seminars in front of the full technical team. Every year there are updates to frames, wheels and components which may require new tools and training for the mechanics. This is especially relevant in the modern era of electric components, which are still relatively new and constantly being improved with hard and software updates.

During this end-of-year period the riders who have been retained by the team will take one of their race bikes home to train on while the newly contracted riders are given one of the team's road bike spares and a time trial bike until they can collect their new bikes built to their exact specifications. Once the new bikes are built up each rider as a minimum will be allocated a race bike plus an identical spare machine and a time trial bike. Star riders will have more road bikes and at least two time trial machines.

That's a lot of new bikes to build prior to the first training camps in the new year and in a week, with all the mechanics working flat out at the team service course, they will build up to 100 machines. Most will be road bikes but there will be time trial bikes, too. Time trial bikes take longer to build. Tri-bars or skis must be cut to exact lengths for each rider and wires and cables have longer and sometimes more complicated runs through the bars and the frame.

The mechanics will also prepare multiple pairs of wheels. They do not build wheels from scratch any more, as they used to, because most wheels with carbon rims are factory built. They will prepare around 50 pairs of new carbon wheels with layers of glue, however, ready for tubular tyre fitting. They may build some training wheels in the traditional style, lacing together rims with a box of spokes and a hub, then trueing the rim by hand with a spoke key, using hand and eye to produce a hand built wheel as good as any other.

That's just the new bikes and wheels at the beginning of the new year, when teams are assembling for training camps in southern Europe and further afield. Media interest is high as fans are eager to see the new team colours and bikes, but after the first batch of bikes are built and the season gets underway in February more machines are built not just to add to the team's regular machines but also for team riders in special events like Strade Bianche and Paris-Roubaix, both of which take place on gravel roads and cobbles.

These bikes may have disc brakes and extra clearances for fatter tyres and even mini suspension units to cope with the impacts and harsh conditions of spring racing. They may only be ridden a few times in the year, and could make a one-off appearance at the Tour de France for a cobbled stage. It explains how, incredibly,

a team of around 30 riders can go through as many as 240 bikes in a full season of pro racing and training.

And some of the most sought after will be the bikes ridden at the Tour de France, which are a mixture of current season and new models often unveiled in races like the Criterium du Dauphine and Tour of Switzerland, both Tour warm-up races which take place in June. As the mechanics are on the road constantly in the months preceding the Tour, some of these machines may be built using the team truck workshop. There is a short window of a week to ten days before the Tour when final bike builds can be completed at the service course, while all the other Tour logistics are finalised before the team heads off their biggest engagement of the year.

◣ New bikes for the Tour are often tested at races like the Criterium du Dauphine in June.

▼ Cobbled races like Paris-Roubaix are raced on special bikes and wheels that may be used again at the Tour.

BIKE BUILD

BIKE BUILD

A new bike build starts with a bare frame, box-fresh, with just the caliper brakes attached and the fork fitted loosely is placed in a bike stand, ideally one in which the front forks are secured and the bottom bracket is also supported. The mechanics may work as a team on bike builds, operating a production line as some jobs, like fitting the 'wiring loom' for the electrics is a delicate and time consuming job best done before the main mechanical build.

The threadless headset bearings are already pressed in but the fork steerer is uncut and needs to be shortened. This can only be done with reference to the rider's bike set-up, which will specify how high the handlebars are positioned. Using a saw guide clamped at the specified steerer length the mechanic takes a hacksaw for carbon parts and saws off the excess length of tube. The guide ensures a square cut. A pipe chamfering tool or file is used to remove rough or sharp edges on the exposed steerer.

The front and rear derailleur mechanisms are then bolted to the rear dropout and front derailleur hanger. The handlebars, either a stem and bars or one-piece integrated bars and stem are fitted to the exposed steerer tube, the top cap fitted and tightened lightly onto the bearing and then the stem bolts tightened.

▲ Preparing cranks with locking compound before assembly.

▶ The service course also functions as a meeting place for the team and its associates.

With the brake levers and calipers and the derailleurs fitted the cables, wires and hydraulic lines are threaded through the ports until all the systems are in place and ready to either be plugged in or fitted. This is one of the most time consuming and intricate tasks of the whole build and may be done before the main mechanical build.

TAILOR MADE

Set-up jigs are used to ascertain the correct position for the brake levers which slide onto the bars ends with their clamps loose but not undone. A jig attached to the end of the bar with sliding horizontal and vertical pieces is set up to make contact with the tip of the brake lever and from here the correct position of the lever on the bars can be set and the lever clamp tightened. All the team's set-up data will be contained either in a note book or on a phone or computer.

With the bottom bracket bearings already pressed in, the chainset and left-hand crank are fitted and the pinch bolts done up to secure the whole chainset in place. If the pedals are not already screwed

▲ At least once every year the mechanics can work in a spacious indoor workshop.

TOUR TIP

Unused equipment from the current season, especially frames which may well have been updated for the following year, can still be built up and used for training at home over the winter and following season.

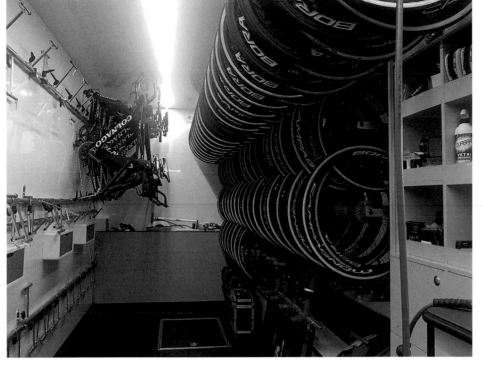

▲ There are new colours every year, even if the bikes are the same.

◀ As the wheels and bikes are completed they are loaded into the truck for the first races of the year.

in they can be fitted at this point. The brake cable outers are also cut to length and taped to the bars. The cables are inserted in the calipers and the pinch bolts done up. Derailleur wires are plugged in using a special tool. If the derailleurs are wireless there are no wires to fit and once batteries are fitted they are ready to go.

With the rear wheel in the bike a new chain is fitted and the front and rear gears set up for the limits of their travel. The battery should already be inserted, often in the seat post and the wires threaded

▼ Building time trial bikes takes longer than road machines.

◀ Custom jigs are used to set up each bike to the rider's exact measurements.

down through the bottom bracket. The junction box can also be fitted integrally or under the stem. With the junction box in the set-up function electronic gears can be adjusted and then checked, running through all the gears on the big and small chainrings. With cable operated gears the fine tuning is done by hand but the run-though checks are the same.

The saddle is fitted and using a jig, the height, angle and fore-aft position can be set for the individual rider. Bottle cages are attached to the down and seat tube. Bar tape is applied and with the front wheel fitted the bike can be checked over on the floor of the workshop, making sure the brakes and pads are correctly adjusted. On disc brakes the calipers will be checked that they do not rub on the rotors and aligned on their mounts if necessary.

The Pinarello F10 X-Light as ridden to victory by Geraint Thomas at the 2018 Tour de France.

CHAPTER 3:

CUSTOM BIKE TECH

From a few metres away, a Tour de France bike, minus the number plate, looks like any other top-of-the-range race bike. A very expensive race bike, it's true, but, as has always been the case with professional racing bikes, the frames and components are mostly mass-produced and available through your local or online bike shop. Look closer, however, and there are numerous tell-tale differences between an authentic Tour bike and a replica machine put together by an enthusiast.

TOUR WINNER'S BIKE

▲ Yellow graphics distinguish the yellow jersey wearer's bike from his teammates at the 2018 Tour.

Geraint Thomas won the 2018 Tour de France on a Pinarello Dogma F10 X-Light fitted with Shimano Dura-Ace Di2 groupset and wheels, with Most bars and stem, a Fizik saddle and Continental tyres. Thomas chose the X-Light for its reduced weight over the regular Dogma F10 frame and although it is not as aerodynamic as other aero road bikes in the Tour, the X-Light is aero in the right places without compromising its ride quality, handling or stability in crosswinds. With wheels built with relatively shallow carbon rims the X-Light proved to be an incredibly light but versatile machine suited to riding at high speed on long flat stages and performing just as impressively during the explosive accelerations of a short mountain stage.

CUT-DOWN SEAT TUBE

The X-Light frame is already lighter and stiffer than the standard F10. Using a lighter carbon fibre and without paint, which can add 100 grams (3½oz), Thomas's 56cm (22in) X-Light frame weighed 760 grams (1¾lb), which with the 330 gram (¾lb) fork, brings the total frame weight to just over one kilogram (2¼lb). It's not the lightest in the peloton and that might explain why the aero seat tube has had a few centimetres cut off from the bottom, to shave a few precious extra grams from the total.

It's not much, maybe 30 grams (1oz), but it illustrates perfectly Team Sky's 'marginal gains' philosophy. Making tiny incremental improvements to every possible component may not, in isolation, amount to a measurable increase in performance but each modification nudges it closer to a measurable gain.

There is also a powerful psychological element to a marginal gain like the cut-down seat tube. In a race like the Tour, where the physical margins between riders at the top of the general classification are wafer thin, the race is won and lost in the heads of the leaders. If a rider believes his mechanic is doing everything possible to tune his bike to be the lightest and fastest it can be, that could make the difference between a winning and losing attack in the final 500 metres (547 yards) of a summit finish.

BATTERY IN THE SEATPOST

Early versions of the Shimano Di2 electronic gears featured an external battery, about the size of a cigarette packet, which was located behind the bottle cage or just in front of the bottom bracket. The battery was exposed to the elements and could be damaged or broken off in a crash. Current versions are cigar shaped and designed to fit inside the frame or, as is the case with the Pinarello, inside the seatpost.

It's a tight fit and some weight is saved by securing the battery with adhesive rather than the internal expander supplied with the battery. To charge the battery the seatpost does not have to be removed, the charger is plugged into the junction box or charging port, located on the down tube or bar end.

To remove the battery it has to be prised out, carefully breaking the seal between the

A. Cut-down seatpost

B. Battery is glued in

C. Seat height sticker

D. Centre of saddle mark

glue and the seatpost. The battery lifetime would almost certainly outlive the seatpost's use to the team and would only be a problem for the next owner.

SEAT HEIGHT STICKER

Seatposts may be removed to replace the battery or sometimes adjusted to suit the rider throughout the race. Normally, the seat height remains unchanged and once it is measured the mechanic will carefully apply a sticker where the seatpost meets the frame to indicate that it has been measured and checked.

A sticker on the tube will also indicate if the seatpost has moved while in use. This can happen all too easily, especially with carbon parts which are fragile and cannot be over-stressed with clamping forces. Many mechanics will apply specialist carbon paste to the seatpost which helps it grip the sides of the seat tube.

SADDLE MARKINGS

The saddle has marks on the top to help the mechanics line-up measuring jigs to guarantee the accuracy of the rider's seat height and distance to the bars. Thomas's seat is pointing slightly down which suits his big gear riding style. Regulations stipulate that the angle of the saddle can only deviate very slightly from the horizontal.

SADDLE CLAMP

This is a special part made by Pinarello and only fitted to a few of their pro rider bikes. Made from titanium and secured with titanium bolts it has an authentically pared-down and rough, prototype or 3D printed look. It's marginally lighter than the stock aluminium clamp but it's worth saving weight above the bike's centre of gravity, especially for a relatively tall rider like Thomas. When you are flying down a mountain pass at 100kph (62mph) it's comforting to know that the mechanics have done everything to make the bike lightning quick through the bends.

BLANKING STICKER

Instead of a plastic blanking plug over the hole where cables would normally go, the team uses stickers which are a few grams lighter. The plastic blanking plug is also secured with a small screw – every gram counts.

REAR GEAR HANGER

Custom-made direct mount gear hangers allow the mechanic to remove a pivoting washer from the rear derailleur which can affect gear change quality and wheel changes. The direct mount gear hanger uses the same 5mm mounting bolt, but without the washer it's a more rigid set-up which improves the precision of the gear change. It also positions the derailleur and jockey wheels a little further back, reducing chain wrap and making wheel changes easier.

E. One-off saddle clamp

F. Sticker replaces plug

G. Custom gear hanger

K-EDGE WASHER

The K-Edge chain catcher is a machined alloy bar which stops the chain coming off the small front chainring, which could put a rider in serious trouble at the moment of a decisive attack. The chain can also damage a carbon fibre frame and the catcher prevents what could be an expensive repair. It also acts as a ramp for the chain, easing the change between rings. On Thomas's bike the washer for a chain catcher is fitted but not the chain catcher itself.

CARBON NUMBER HOLDER

No part, however small, escapes the attention of the mechanics if they think a few grams can be saved, or spared. There are parts of the bike, like the frame, the bars and wheels, which may not be as light as alternative brands but, other than

stripping them of paint for instance, nothing is done which might negatively affect the strength of the component. Attention is turned to anything which can be lightened which does not affect the integrity or safety of the bike.

In the case of a custom-made number hanger, instead of a piece of aluminium sheet, carbon fibre is used and even the number itself is trimmed, although the organisers could take a dim view of any tampering with something with a sponsor's branding on it. Each rider is supplied with enough numbers for all his race and spare bikes in the Tour.

The number hanger had been fitted behind the brake but there was a risk of it compressing when the brake bolt was tightened, making the brake move slightly in use. Moving it to the seat clamp was a neat and safe solution.

H. Silver K-Edge washer

I. Carbon number holder

TRANSPONDER

Like the race number, the transponder is a requirement for all riders in the Tour and is used to trip the timer when it crosses the finish line. There is not much that the mechanic can do other than fit it securely to the chainstay. Under this transponder there is a small strip of grip tape to hold it more securely against the stay.

UNDER SEAT TRACKER

Supplied by Dimension Data to all the Tour teams, the tracker transmits speed and position and can be displayed on TV or used to determine exact distances between groups of riders. They have been used for a few years at the Tour and are charged by the team every three or four days.

BAR TAPE

Riders have their own preferences for bar tape and Thomas's is very light and has a comfortable brushed finish. Wrapping is very neat and at the centre of the bars the end of the tape has been glued rather than finished with a few turns of electrical masking tape. Mechanics change bar tape every day at the Tour but not on every bike, just the ones which are scuffed or dirty. It takes more care to glue the tape but it looks good and is another finishing touch which sets a team leader's bike apart from the rest.

QUICK-RELEASE SKEWERS

On the inside of the quick-release lever a '5' is marked by hand in felt tip. When the bikes are loaded in the morning some

J. Tour de France transponder

K. Saddle-mounted tracker

L. Bar ribbon glued

will have their front wheels removed. The number corresponds to the rider's race number and it is important that the correct front wheels arc fitted to each bike, as the tyre pressure will have been set for each individual. The leader's bike will often be loaded as a complete machine and this front wheel is not an '8' and must have been fitted after the race.

YELLOW DETAILING

Up until Thomas won the yellow jersey on stage 11 his bike featured standard Pinarello Dogma F10 X-Light graphics in white. But when he was in yellow the bike's white graphics were very carefully overlaid with laser cut yellow replicas, slightly smaller than the originals which make them stand out better against a white outline. Up close the yellow graphics are peeling in places, possibly after jet washing after each stage. The team has the stickers made before the Tour and the mechanics will have spent an extra half-hour or so carefully applying them the night after the yellow jersey was taken.

NAME AND NUMBER STICKERS

Thomas has his name and small Welsh flag on a sticker applied to the top tube just in front of the seatpost. This helps the mechanics and the rider identify the bike at a glance, which matters when there are eight bikes ridden at the start of the stage and another eight spare machines on top of the team car. Of course, only one bike in the whole peloton gets the yellow sticker upgrade which, admittedly, does make identification of this machine somewhat easier!

The small number one sticker denotes this as Thomas's number one machine

for the stage it has been prepared for. His second bike would be on the team car roof, on the outside where the mechanic can grab it faster than any of the other spares. A rider like Thomas will have come to the Tour with three road bikes and two time trial machines. Each of the road bikes will be numbered and if the number one bike is not involved in a crash it will stay as the rider's first bike throughout the race.

M. Numbered QR lever

N. Yellow graphics

O. Welsh dragon sticker

Every Tour mechanic has his own personalised toolbox, usually in a hard case with multiple sections.

CHAPTER 4:

ESSENTIAL TOOLKIT

Every professional mechanic at the Tour de France has his own favourite tools and whenever you see a toolbox opened, with personalised stickers and ranks of well-used tools inside, you know that the owner will not be far away and is guarding jealously his most treasured possessions. There are general tools for use by all the mechanics on a team but the personal tools are particular to each individual, with a mixture of the basic and the exotic, they are to the mechanic what brushes are to the portrait painter.

GENERAL TOOLS

▲ Hex keys and all types of screwdriver are the most commonly used tools.

A. Standard hex keys

B. Hex drivers

C. Hex multi-tool

D. T-handle hex tools

E. Socket set

F. Standard torque wrench

G. Small torque wrench with hex and Torx bits

H. Single torque bike keys

I. Small torque wrench

HEX KEYS

Hex or Allen bolts are the most widely used fasteners on a bike. Every home mechanic has a set of tools for these bolts either made up of individual keys or as part of a multi-tool. The most common sizes are 4, 5 and 6mm and are used for components like bars and stems, seatposts and brakes, which require regular checks and adjustments. Lesser quality steel and sloppy machining can damage bolts or the key heads, both resulting in rounded-out bolts which over time can become difficult or impossible to turn.

A hex key is the most common tool you are likely to see a Tour mechanic using and for this reason they want the very best that money can buy. A set of basic L-shaped keys are essential, usually comprising up to ten individual keys from 1.5mm to 10mm. Ideally one end will have a conventional hex end while the other will have the ball style hex which allows the tool to be turned at a slight angle to the bolt. It's also very handy if each key is clearly identified, by colour for instance, making selection of the correct size hex faster and safer. It can be tricky to tell the 4mm from the 5mm and if your keys are not colour coded a piece of different coloured insulating tape tightly applied around each does the same job.

T-HANDLE HEX TOOLS

Many mechanics will also have a set of soft T-handle hex keys, with one head at the end of a long bar and a short stubby one set into one side of the handle. These are the tools with their coloured plastic handles you will

often see hanging in the tool case of each individual mechanic and show all the signs of regular use.

Sliding T-handle keys are less likely to be found in the home toolbox but are favoured by pro mechanics who value their versatility and extra leverage over an L-shaped key. Made from hardened steel bar, one end has a hex end while the other has a slot through which a short double-ended hex bar can slide. Each end of the top of the T is a different size and can either be used on bolts with the long bar exerting varying levels of torque, or using the T as the handle, often for winding in bolts from a few millimetres out.

HEX BITS AND TORX BOLTS

There is a third type of hex key which can be fixed or inserted like a drill bit into a torque wrench and is intended for use on crushable and delicate parts typically made from carbon fibre. These hex bits are a few centimetres long and would normally be used for bolts on carbon handlebars and stems and seatposts in carbon frames.

Some hex tools have a hex head at one end and a Torx head on the other. Common in automotive applications the flat, six-head Torx head fastener grips the tool better than a hex and is designed for higher loadings. That is not normally an issue for bikes but the flat head is useful for certain components which require relatively tight or flush-fitting bolts on components, like disc rotors, brake lever mounts, caliper brake pads and gear hanger mounts. Torx bolts are also lighter thanks to their flatter heads and as the price comes down could be used more widely on race bikes. To avoid the risk of overtightening it's advisable to use a Torx bit with a bike specific

▲ A useful three-bit hex tool ideal for stage starts.

A. Scissors

B. Cutters various

C. Cable cutter

D. Box cutter

E. Screwdrivers various

F. Adjustable wrench various

G. Mole grips

H. Pliers various

I. Plier wrench

torque wrench either pre-set or adjustable. Typical Torx head sizes for bikes are T10, T25 and T30.

MULTI-TOOL

There is one more hex tool which every mechanic will have close to hand, or in his pocket. A small multi-tool with half a dozen or so hex keys is always to hand when the mechanic is away from his tool case or the mobile workshop. Because there is always a bolt to check or a small adjustment to be made by a rider minutes before the stage, or even during it!

CUTTERS

Relatively inexpensive, cable cutters were a toolbox essential, though less frequently used thanks to the almost universal take-up of non-cable-operated electronic gear systems. Hydraulic disc brakes are also non-cable operated but traditional caliper brakes remain popular and cables, the inner steel and outer housing too, require cutting to precise lengths for each frame. Precision ground cutting jaws are designed to wrap around the cable ensuring the wound steel strands do not splay when cut. The exposed cable is protected with a soft alloy cable end cap and good cable cutters also incorporate crimpers for end cables and ferrules which go on the end of cable outers.

Cable cutters are not suitable for hydraulic brake hoses made of tougher plastic; these are cut using a hose cutter with an integral sharp blade. An additional needle driver tool is used to ream out the exposed end of the hose. Pro mechanics may also have a precision wire cutter to shorten or modify electrical cables found on the electronic gear systems.

Every mechanic will also have a quality pair of scissors for cutting and trimming items like bar tape and plastic race numbers. They will also have a box cutter or Stanley knife for trimming and scraping.

SCREWDRIVERS

Flat-headed screws are rarely used on modern race bikes but cross-headed ones are still found on derailleurs where they are used to stop the mechanism from exceeding the limits of its inboard and outboard throws. Small cross-head screws may also be used to attach plastic computer and head unit brackets to handlebars or stems. These little screw heads are notoriously easy to damage or round-out and a little known reason is because they are often made to the Japanese Industrial Standard (JIS) head measurement which is slightly different to the Phillips head. A pro mechanic will have at least one JIS head screwdriver for those screws found on Japanese-made gear systems and any other bracket or Japanese accessory. You may have to hunt around for one but it's worth having a JIS screwdriver in your home toolbox.

PLIER WRENCH

Not the most obvious tool for a pro bicycle mechanic, the plier wrench may look like a traditional monkey wrench, but a precision version can take the place of the adjustable spanner. These wrenches are smaller than a plumber's and their finely cast jaws and adjustment ratchet mechanism are reflected in the price. Doing the same job as an adjustable spanner, which can be used on any size of nut or removal tool, the wrench is quicker to adjust and more secure. Not a tool which would be used very often if at all on

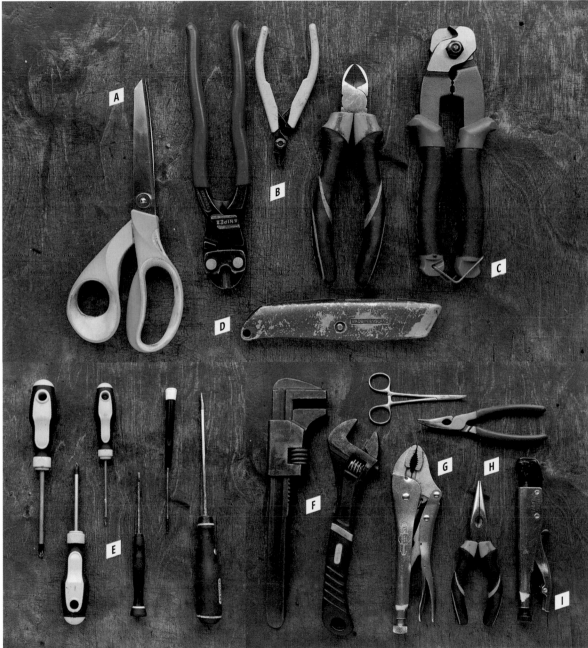

the bike itself, the plier wrench is nevertheless one of those all-round essentials which can be called up for the removal of cassettes or for help turning headset and bottom bracket fitting tools and parts. An adjustable wrench is still likely to be found in a pro mechanic's toolbox, however, as they remain a great all-round tool for a variety of larger nuts not found on the bike, from bicycle measuring jigs to headset and bottom bracket tools.

A

TYRE PRESSURE GAUGES

Regular cyclists pump up their tyres with a track or stirrup pump and use the integral gauge to achieve the desired pressure in psi or bar. That is absolutely fine for most riders but for pro racing and of course the Tour, where every team is looking for a tiny advantage, the battle is now fought down to the last psi.

There is a tyre pressure calculation to be made every day of the Tour, usually depending on the chance of rain or the condition of the roads, both of which might lead to a slight reduction in tyre pressures. The same goes for stages with cobbles, which sees the mechanics working from bike to bike checking off lower pressures for each rider depending on their weight and riding style.

Introduced for cyclo-cross racing, where there is an obsessive attention to tyre pressures, tyre pressure gauges for bikes with Presta style valves are the only way

to measure accurately the air pressure in the tube. Custom-made digital gauges are available featuring proprietary Presta nozzles attached to a gauge with digital readout. There's a bleed valve allowing the mechanic to see the pressure reduce as air is leaked out. This type of gauge is incredibly accurate compared to the five psi plus or minus of a track pump.

CASSETTE WRENCH

A cassette removal tool is a big nut with a splined end which slots into the cassette body. To remove the cassette the quick-release has to come out and the tool inserted securely or clamped in place. A big spanner or adjustable wrench is used on the tool to undo the cassette while the mechanic simultaneously stops the sprockets turning with a chain whip or toothed wrench.

As this is not a task that many cyclists will tackle more than a few times a year it does not matter that it takes a few minutes of careful setting up to remove a cassette. A Tour mechanic removes cassettes every day and, with eight or more machines to

A. Digital tyre pressure gauge

B. Chain whip

C. Cassette wrench

B

C

work on, he prizes any tool which saves time and effort. The custom cassette removal tool looks simple and it is, comprised of the correct size splined insert attached to a handle. This removes the need for a separate spanner which has to be fitted securely over the cassette tool nut and can all too easily and frustratingly slip off.

Another time saving innovation is the oversize hollow end designed to slip over the end of the quick-release, which can remain in place throughout the removal of the cassette. Like the best custom tools it is simple but ingenious. The mechanic still needs to lock the sprockets manually and another custom tool, with three teeth which fit between the sprocket teeth around the cassette, is also easier to use than the traditional chain whip.

TAPS

A selection of taps from 2.5 to 10mm are useful for refreshing threads on worn parts like gear hangers. A similar tool but less aggressive on the threads is used for chasing out or cleaning a thread which may have paint or compacted grease and dirt in it.

CARBON FIBRE TOOLS

Great care is needed when cutting carbon fibre tubes and steerers as they can splinter and throw up noxious dust if done with inappropriate tools. A carbon fibre specific hacksaw should guarantee a clean cut with the minimum of dust and a clamp with a cutting saw guide will ensure the cut is clean and perfectly square. From a plumber's toolbox, the pipe finisher is an ingenious and simple device which looks like a small

D. Standard hacksaws

E. Wet and dry paper

F. Cutting saw guides

G. Files

H. Carbon saw

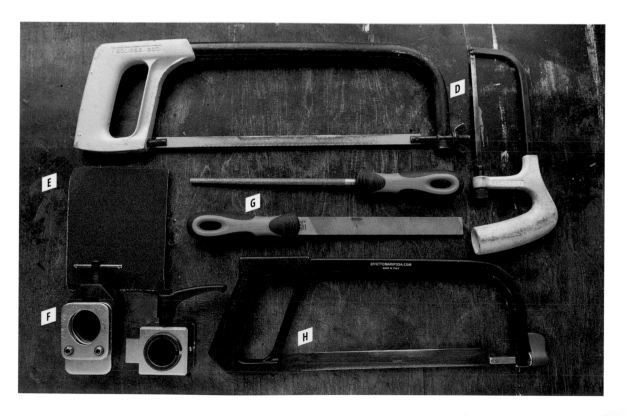

▲ Used water bottles make handy glue applicators for fitting tubular tyres.

plastic cup. Inside the cup are triple steel cutters, concave on one side and convex on the other. When placed over the rough end of a pipe the tool is turned by hand and removes burrs on the inside and outside edge of the cut bar. Essential for tidying up the sharp ends of carbon handlebars, tri-bars and steerers.

TUBULAR TYRE GLUEING

One of the few labour intensive and laborious yet skilled jobs undertaken by the Tour mechanics, preparing rims and glueing on tubular tyres is a two-part operation with a few basic tools. Emery cloth or a fine wire bush is used to key the lacquer on new carbon rims, while a file can be used to remove a thin layer of glue on the inside of the tubular tyre itself. Rims with layers of

old glue also need to be rubbed down with a wire brush or even pared back using a short bladed knife. For glueing, some tubular glue pots have an integral brush but if not a small flat-headed paint brush is used to apply thin layers of glue. Glue can also be applied in blobs, from an old cycling or squeezy sauce bottle. All these preparing and glueing jobs are easier if the wheel is mounted in a jig for trueing wheels.

FORK DROPOUT

Spare wheels are carried on and inside team cars, ready for fast wheel changes in the event of a puncture. To minimise the time spent fitting the wheel by the side of the road the mechanic uses a fork dropout on each spare wheel to screw each quick-release clamp into the same position, saving

I. Pick sets various

J. Cables and bob weight

valuable seconds. This tool cannot be used on forks with through axles.

MAGNET

A small magnet on the end of a flexible shaft is very useful for picking up dropped fasteners, especially if they have disappeared into the hollow recesses of a carbon fibre frame.

BENT WIRES, HOOK AND PICK SETS, AND PLIERS

Integrating cables, wires, batteries and other functions has created many fiddly tasks routing these systems inside frames and components. Pro mechanics have their own favourites but all need to have a selection of tools for locating, finding and pulling through cables, clips and batteries. Delicate

operations like removing circlips and dust caps, or accessing battery retaining clips require a pair of bent nose pliers. Batteries located in down tubes, seat tubes and other inaccessible places can be difficult to remove for charging and checks. Rubber handled hook and pick tools can also be very useful for teasing out cables, and if all else fails the good old wire coat hanger can be a life saver.

LAPTOP

Laptops are now almost an essential tool for every mechanic as there are many electronic components which can be programmed and analysed. Electronic gear systems can be programmed in multiple configurations ranging from the speed of the shift to the individual function of each button. Apps on phones and head units

▼ Notebooks filled with rider and bike set-ups have been replaced by laptops that are also used to programme e-components.

can also be used to access the functions of the control units on electric gears. It's not just programming that a mechanic may have a laptop for. He may well use it to store detailed information on each rider on the team relating to bike set-up and any relevant kit or gear preferences. Modern bike-fit systems generate a lot more data than traditional methods, which were not much more than saddle height, reach to the bars and measurement of the seat behind the bottom bracket.

MASKING TAPE

One of the simplest things in the toolbox, but essential for making a note of anything and sticking it to the relevant part of the bike. Before a cobbled stage, for instance, every machine may have masking tape on the top tube with individual tyre pressures front and back for each of the eight team bikes. When you are working on multiple machines it is all too easy to make a mental note to do something and then forget to do it. Even the home mechanic may leave a job half-finished and then forget to finish

it at a later date. A piece of paper-based masking tape, which doesn't damage the paintwork, is a handy reminder.

DIGITAL SCALES

No bike in the Tour is allowed to weigh less than 6.8kg (15lb) and the world governing body polices its rules on randomly selected bikes throughout the Tour. Weight limits and the dimensions of bikes, especially time trial machines, are the responsibility of the mechanics and explains why they are fanatical about achieving weights and frame and bar parameters as close to the limit as possible.

WATERPROOFS

Not just wellies, pro mechanics at the Tour have to work outside in all weathers, even in July. A full set of waterproofs and boots will not only keep out the rain, they make washing multiple bikes and wheels considerably more tolerable. Even for the home mechanic, waterproof rubber boots and even rubber gloves are worth putting on when washing bikes.

▶ Every storage space on the truck is filled with essential kit for maintaining and washing bikes.

▶▶ A robust workshop apron and waterproof shoes will keep the worst off when washing and working on bikes after the stage.

Riders may get most of the accolades, but without the hard work of a diverse team behind them, they'd be nowhere.

CHAPTER 5:

INSIDE THE TEAM

Behind every team of eight riders is a small army of support crew dedicated to keeping the show, literally, on the road. Sport directors, a doctor, a cook, masseurs and all-round helpers can be seen busy at work whenever the team de-camps during the Tour. It is an impressive sight to see these tight-knit units about their work at the start and finish of each stage. Among the most visible and popular among the wandering fans, are the team mechanics.

INSIDE THE TEAM
THE MECHANICS

▲ Two mechanics work from the truck while two are in the team cars.

World Tour and Pro-Continental teams bring their finest riders to the Tour de France. They also bring their best mechanics, usually four from a team of up to nine. Ages vary, from older mechanics with decades of experience to younger men with all the skills and the energy to put in long hours over the three-week race. While women do make up some of the staff on a pro team, they have yet to break into the male world of pro bike racing mechanics. Working on the Tour is the highlight of any mechanic's year but with the prestige and pressure comes long days working on bikes before and after stages as well as performing mobile servicing from team cars during each stage.

Mechanics come from all sorts of backgrounds. There is no internationally accepted route into becoming a pro team accredited mechanic. Each individual will have learned the basics either by working on their own bikes as former bike racers, or in bike shops in their home countries. They will have probably gained a qualification in bicycle shop mechanics and will have the third party insurance required to work on customer bikes. A mechanic with an excellent reputation might be picked up directly from a local bike shop by a pro team but a more likely route would be from working on a smaller team beforehand.

Having an interest, or preferably an obsession, in bike racing helps. Many pro team bike mechanics have either raced at amateur or even pro level and experienced life on the road with all its ups and downs. The internationalisation of cycling in the last 30 years has transformed the peloton and the same can be said of the support staff, including the mechanics. Gone are the days when only mechanics from the team's host nation worked at the Tour. Mechanics come from both sides of the Atlantic and each one has their own story to tell about how they got their dream job.

What makes a Tour de France mechanic, apart from the ability to work miracles on a bike? It varies, of course, but most mechanics will say they love the travel and working as part of a team. Working on bikes in a shop or at home can be a solitary existence which suits some but the Tour mechanic must be someone who relishes the dynamics of working with other mechanics and also as part of the greater team. Only team players are picked for a race like the Tour – a selfish individual will soon be found out among a small group who live and work together 24/7 over three weeks.

There may have been a time when the Tour mechanic was a less than fit looking individual, spotted at work with a cigarette in one hand and a spanner in the other. In the pre-modern era when the Tour was smaller and teams were equipped with fewer bikes, the job of the mechanic may have been just as time consuming, but there was certainly less interaction with the public or with sponsors and suppliers. In the modern era the mechanics are almost as well known as the riders! They work in hotel car parks and race start and finish areas surrounded by crowds fascinated to see the machines and mechanics working on them. They are part of the show and that could be why many of them take a lot more care over their appearance and levels of fitness!

The Tour is the most important month of the year for team sponsors and associates to showcase their bikes and components. Mechanics these days are expected to take time to talk to both the public and sponsors at the Tour. They must also be on hand to co-operate with every type of media request and keep a proprietorial eye on machines being photographed for websites and magazines. On rest days they may be asked to check over bikes ridden by corporate visitors and will even tweak a local rider's bike if he is going for a spin with the team. But there is one thing they will not appreciate being asked. Do not expect a Tour mechanic to lend you anything – the golden rule of all pro mechanics is never lend out your precious tools.

Mechanics work on more than the team's racing bikes. They are also responsible for setting up each rider's shoe plates, as well as cleaning them and washing helmets. They will be called into action for anything that can be fixed on the team vehicles, from bike racks to changing wheels and minor crash damage. Tour mechanics are the most versatile team players and that could be why they are invariably the type of person with an upbeat personality and a robust sense of humour.

▼ After changing a wheel, the mechanic gives the rider a big running shove to get him going again.

TEAM TRUCK

From the outside the team truck looks much like any other commercial heavy goods vehicle. The team colours, sponsor and rider names on the body give the game away to the fan, but on a motorway a team truck could pass unnoticed among their fellow frozen fish and furniture carrying wagons in the slow lane. Team cars rocket along in the fast lane in a blaze of colourful logos, bikes and with wheels on roof racks glittering in the light. The team bus with its blacked out windows contains an air of mystery as it wafts a team of superstar riders to and from stages. No one see the team truck as it noses into the hotel car park, looking like it's making a humdrum delivery to the kitchens.

Until the tailgate opens. Loitering fans look on in awe at the array of bikes and wheels inside the most tightly packed dream bikeshop-cum-workshop on the road. Steps glide out, awnings extend and more doors open to reveal an additional workspace behind the cab. Team personnel busy themselves, not just the mechanics assembling workstands and tools outside the truck but also the team carers and helpers appear with bags of food, laundry and further supplies for load bays and storage cupboards. Only one person is not enthralled by all this fascinating activity around a Tardis-like truck. A slightly

▼ Every team has a big truck that opens up to reveal all the stored bikes, tools and spares.

bored-looking security guard keeps a practised eye over the milling fans and expensive kit spilling out of the truck. His job really starts later, when all the bikes are packed away for the night and a break-in, sadly all-too possible in recent times, would be catastrophic for a team at the Tour de France.

Not only is the team truck the beating heart of the team, it is also the team's most valuable rolling asset. On board there can be up to 50 bikes in the main storage area and 120 pairs of wheels. Just the bikes and wheels can be worth half a million pounds. Add to that up to 100 new tubular tyres, drawers full of boxed spares and specialist tools and the value of the bikes and parts alone represents a significant part of the team's annual budget. That explains why deterring theft has become a serious consideration for all Tour de France teams in the modern era.

Forward of the main storage area, where the bikes and wheels are hung up and stacked, is a smaller cabin just behind the cab where the team's mobile kitchen and laundry are located. In here is a washer and dryer for cleaning the kit of all eight cyclists after each stage. A grab bag is collected from each rider every evening and exchanged for clean kit the next day. In the kitchen there is a big fridge as well as storage cupboards full of energy food, tasty fillings and snacks and drinks, all for consumption before, during and after the stage. One of the bigger storage units is used for the rider's bottles, hundreds of which are used over three weeks. Bottles are not neatly stacked like everything else in the truck, there are too many of

them. They are poured like grains of rice into a big storage box and grabbed as they tumble from a hatch at the bottom. In underfloor lockers down the sides of the truck is where bottled water and soft drinks are stored. If there is room, turbo trainers may also be found here but every truck is different and each team has their own preferred systems.

At the back of the truck the tailgate offers some shelter from the elements and steps see plenty of traffic as mechanics come and go with bikes and spares. There are enough spares to run a small bike shop here, with cassettes and chainrings hanging up for easy access and in the drawers, packed with everything from complete groupsets to consumables like brake pads and chains in plentiful numbers. Bigger tools, bike building and measuring jigs are also stowed in the truck as well as a compressor used for inflating tyres and drying components. All trucks are now wired up with dozens of power points used to charge electronic gears, which are plugged in after each stage.

Most of the work on bikes is done with the bikes on workstands around the back of the truck but there is at least one workbench with a trusty vice if a hard surface is required for working on individual parts or jobs, such as cutting steerers and bars. Not many trucks have enough space for the mechanics to work inside and at the Tour de France they are often found sweating in the late afternoon sun, washing bikes and preparing them for the following day's stage. If it's raining, awnings keep the worst off but mechanics cannot stray too far from the mothership.

▲ Wheels for every stage type and weather condition are racked in the team truck.

TEAM CAR

▲ The mechanic just has room to sit beside his tools and spare wheel in the team car.

Each of the 22 teams in the Tour de France has two team cars following the race on every road stage. One of the cars is given a sticker which goes on the back window and denotes its position in the line of team cars behind the bunch. The number is blue or black and represents the position of the team's highest placed rider on general classification. The team of the yellow jersey is car number one, the second placed rider overall is car number two and so on.

The second team car is given the same numbers, but in red, relating to their top rider on GC. All the team's second cars line up in the same order behind the first team cars, after car number 22. That makes 44 team cars behind the bunch at the start of the race. In total, including team officials, medics, neutral service and police there are about 65 vehicles (plus about 30 motorbikes) behind the bunch at the start of the race. When the break goes away the race organiser calls up the number two team cars for riders represented in the break. They pass the peloton and form up behind the break, again in GC rider order.

In each team is a sports director behind the wheel, another sports director or possibly doctor in the passenger seat and a mechanic in the back seat. There are bikes and spare wheels on the roof. Inside are more spare wheels and the rest of the car, in every possible storage and cubby hole, is stuffed with cooler bags with bottles, race food, wet weather bags and telecoms to communicate with the riders, the other team car and the race radio. There are

also monitors for watching the race from the live TV feed. The team car is a rolling command centre, quartermasters stores and pitstop in one vehicle.

On the custom-made roof racks a team car can typically carry four complete bikes, four bikes without front wheels and six spare front and rear wheels. It's a tight fit for all this kit and for that reason the spare machines for highest placed riders or team leaders are always clamped on the outside of the rack, not overlapping wheels with the other bikes and within the easiest reach of the mechanic when he jumps out of the car. Of the eight man team, the top four have complete bikes as spares and the other four riders have bikes in the centre of the rack which will need a front wheel to be fitted in the event of a bike change. Inside the car, alongside the mechanic on the back seat are more spare wheels, usually two fronts and two rears.

It's particularly cramped on the back seat of a team car, where the mechanic installs himself and must remain alert for the duration of a stage. Not only does he have to be ready to jump out and change a wheel after a puncture, he is also in charge of a big cool box full of bottles, cans of drink and ice cubes. On hot days the ice cubes are put into women's stockings bundled up in the door cubbies and handed out to riders, who shove them down the back of their jerseys.

This is done through the window while moving along, as are various mechanical and clothing fixes which the mechanic is expected to perform. With the rider alongside the car in the race convoy the mechanic might be called upon to fix his radio, adjust gears and brakes, change shoes and helmets and bodge a crash repair. For this reason it helps if the stage mechanic is fit and flexible. He also needs to have nerves of steel.

Each mechanic has his own personalised heavy-duty tool case but they also have a portable version, sometimes in a soft case, which they take with them on their days in the team car. These lighter bags contain all the tools required for in-race adjustments and fixes. There may also be a more complete tool kit on the boot of the car for those days in every Tour when the team car doubles as a mobile disaster recovery unit after multiple crashes or unforeseen damage to a bike. There is a limit to what can be achieved in such a tight space though.

On the headrest in front of the mechanic is a monitor with a live feed from the race TV and he will also be able to hear the race radio calling up team cars to assist riders or more urgently, to announce a puncture or crash. Now that riders are in direct contact with the team car through their race radios that can also give the mechanic precious extra seconds to prepare for a wheel change. Also on the headrest is a schematic of the bikes on the roof, again to help the mechanic locate the correct spare bike as quickly as possible. In the door cubby there will always be oil for chains and grease or an aerosol can for more lubing options. Somewhere there is a pump, manual or pneumatic – the cyclist's number one portable friend is never far away.

▼ A team car loaded with time trial bikes will still have a mechanic in the back as it follows each rider during his solo effort.

Every day is busy and long for Tour team mechanics at the Tour de France.

CHAPTER 6:

A DAY IN THE LIFE OF A TOUR MECHANIC

Tour de France mechanics are among the hardest working people on the three-week race. Up early every day and rarely finished before nightfall, the four mechanics on each team are its backbone, working tirelessly to keep the show on the road. There is a routine to every mechanic's day but on the Tour, there is no such thing as a regular day at the office.

A DAY IN THE LIFE OF A TOUR MECHANIC

▲ A rider may want to discuss a bike-related issue before the start.

Tour de France mechanics are among the hardest working people on the three-week race. Up early every day and rarely finished before nightfall, the four mechanics on each team are its backbone, toiling diligently to keep the show on the road with unflappable good humour. There is a routine to every mechanic's day but on the Tour de France, there is no such thing as a regular day at the office.

No matter what happened the previous day, which may have brought the euphoria of a stage win or a miserable time of punctures, crashes and abandons, a new day at the Tour always brings fresh hope of success. From the eight riders on each team to the sports managers, carers, bus driver and the four mechanics, the ability to roll with the punches thrown by a grand tour is what sets them apart from ordinary mortals.

The mechanics might have spent the previous day working late into the night repairing and rebuilding bikes damaged in crashes, or methodically scraping rims and applying glue for new tyres after a spate of punctures. On the morning of a new stage the same mechanics will be up and about by seven in the morning, even on a day when the stage does not start until midday, not uncommon with the shorter stages of the modern Tour.

0700–0800 HOURS

After a quick breakfast in the hotel buffet, the first job of the mechanics is to open up the team truck which may have been securely parked overnight. Thieves have been known to empty team trucks of bikes and kit and it has been necessary in recent years for teams and races like the Tour to block the rear doors of their team trucks and provide a night watchman in the hotel car park. Once the truck is opened up, the eight bikes on which the team is due to start the stage are loaded onto one of the spare team car or van roof racks. Eight spare machines and additional spare wheels are also loaded. If the stage start is only a few kilometres away the team may ride there on their bikes, in which case the tyres are pumped up at the hotel and the bikes are lined up against the truck. Normally there is a drive to the start, which can easily be an hour or more, especially once the team buses and cars hit race traffic. The Tour is so big that only large towns and cities have enough hotels to lodge the teams a few kilometres from a stage start.

0800–0900 HOURS

At the hotel the team cars are driven out in search of fuel and set up for the day's stage. This will include taking out the relevant pages and information about the stage from the Tour's official roadbook. Not available to fans, the race manual is the bible of every race follower. Apart from detailed route information and timings based on various average speeds for every stage, the book also contains essential maps for the starts and finishes showing team entry and exit routes in and out of the secure starts and finishes.

There can be four cars per team, plus the bus carrying the riders heading off to the start. Times that by 22 and that's 110 team vehicles alone converging on an area

◄ On the bus to the start, the riders relax and prepare for the stage while the mechanics drive to the start in team cars.

set aside for the teams to assemble before each stage. As well as the teams there are the official race cars and motorbikes, the police motorbikes and all the press and TV cars and motorbikes – the daily traffic of the Tour is enough to cause gridlock in a medium sized town.

To avoid what would be absolute chaos if all these vehicles were left to find their own way to the start, the race manual's most important page for the teams is probably the map which shows exactly the point at which they must enter the policed route to each day's stage start. This is known as the PPO (Point de Passage Obligatoire) and every team vehicle will have the PPO programmed into their GPS and will be looking out for the big red and white PPO sign which denotes the entry point, usually on the outskirts of the stage town. All the drivers, especially the bus and the mechanics in the team cars breathe a small sigh of relief when they see the

PPO as they know they are on the correct route into the stage start and should have about an hour till the start to get the riders to the signing-on stage and the bikes ready for the stage.

0900–1100 HOURS

Once the team convoy of up to half a dozen vehicles has found its way to the official route into the stage start, signs with a yellow roundel and a P on it direct the teams to an area or road big enough to park up next to all the other teams. There are different coloured temporary signs directing all accredited Tour vehicles to zones set aside for race officials, the race publicity caravan, media and invitees.

Some are located so that the vehicles can move off in front of the race and some are in side-roads and car parks behind, moving off after the peloton has rolled over the linc. This is where the team parking is located, with the team cars assembling behind the bunch in the final minutes before the roll out. After the start the empty team buses and any team vehicles not following the stage leave the start zone and take the shortest non-race route to the stage finish to set up and await the riders.

In the area for team parking (Parking Equipes) each team is directed to a space big enough for all the vehicles, where the two mechanics on that day's stage duty get out and set up temporary barriers to allow the fans to see the riders and bikes without getting in their way. This is the Tour, there will already be hundreds of fans in the team parking area, many of them ready to descend upon their favourite teams and riders.

The riders are on the bus and will come out now and again to check something on the bikes and then en masse when they ride to the signing-on stage. In the meantime the mechanics are the centre of attention as they unload the day's eight bikes to be ridden from the start from a team vehicle and put them in stands in front of the team bus.

There will already be air in the tyres of all the bikes and spare wheels but the number one machines will be checked with digital tyre pressure gauges and topped up if necessary. On a normal flat stage in the dry the regular tyre pressures are often very similar for each rider but on stages with rough roads or especially cobbles, when higher volume tyres are used, there could be specific inflation pressures for each bike front and rear.

That would be based on rider weight and preferences for how the tyres feel on the harsh cobbles. On a stage with cobbles,

▶ Riders and mechanics share a close working relationship and are often friends.

the mechanics will stick masking tape to the top tubes of each bike with the tyre pressures in felt tip for both front and rear tyres. They will also have hex keys to hand for any last minute adjustments to the bars and stem, seatpost or saddle. Few mechanics can pass a bike without double-checking a bolt here and there. It is not unusual for a rider to emerge from the team bus and, after finding his bike in the line-up, ask the mechanic to alter the position by a millimetre or two. Some riders are notorious for making tiny adjustments, others just hop on and ride the bike with their name on the top tube. A rider who has crashed or may be carrying an injury may also want to tweak a component to alleviate a niggling issue when in the saddle. Team mechanics are always ready for a last minute panic adjustment, when the rider feels something is not right after pedalling to the signing-on.

1100–1300 HOURS

After double-checking the tyres and making sure the number one bikes all have their numbers and transponders securely fixed, the mechanics put water bottles into the bikes and fix computers and head units in mounts. They may also be double-checking that all the batteries are displaying a full charge on the battery life indicator module under the stem. The machines are ready for the stage and await their riders to descend from the bus, but still the mechanics fuss over them. An obsessive attention to the tyres, which may have been ridden over gravel to the signing-on, continues as they wipe them down with a rag. A puncture before the start is detested as a spare wheel will have to be

used, leaving one less replacement tyre before a pedal is turned in anger.

Brakes are another component that mechanics and riders are constantly fiddling with. Riders descend from the team bus and before they clip into their machines they try the brakes, checking that they come on smoothly and that both pads contact the rim at the same time. With disc brakes they may lift the front and spin the wheel to check that the pads are not dragging. In both cases there will be a mechanic hovering nearby with a tool to realign a caliper. Before they do this they may also undo and reapply the quick-release, ensuring that the wheel is centred in the dropouts.

1300–1700 HOURS

Each of the two team cars on the race has a mechanic lodged between spare wheels and tools on the back seat. The other two mechanics on the team drive the truck with all the essential tools and spare bikes and kit to the hotel allocated to the team at the end of the stage. How long it takes to drive to the hotel can depend on many factors from the length of the stage and accessibility of connecting motorways, to the distance of the hotel from the stage finish. In remote areas with few hotels the team can be faced with an extra hour's drive or so after some stages.

Once the truck arrives at the hotel, the two mechanics will set up an area in the car park, hook up electrics and hoses and prepare the washing and tools for cleaning and servicing the bikes used on the stage. If there is time they will apply glue to wheels for tubular tyres, build up or repair

▲ Fine-tuning is a never-ending job for the Tour mechanic.

▲ The team car leaves after the stage and goes directly to the hotel.

spare machines with new components and prepare time trial or specialist bikes for an upcoming stage.

In the team car the mechanics take their place not knowing if there is a quiet day ahead or a stage featuring multiple punctures or crashes. An uneventful day will still almost certainly involve some activity from the back seat, even if it is just a single wheel change after a puncture, a minor adjustment to a rider's gears or brakes on the move, or handing up a bottle or handful of ice cubes in a stocking to cool the riders on a hot day.

Mechanics get used to leaning out of the window of the team car and there are no harnesses to stop them falling out. Apart from mechanical issues, they may have to fiddle with a rider's radio or help him change a helmet or even a shoe, all on the move. With a star rider holding onto the car at 45kph (28mph) it takes a cool head and very steady hands to perform these tasks, and rarely do riders crash – such is the skill of all parties involved. These actions may take a stressful minute or two. A typical 200km (124 miles) flat stage can take five hours and it's not unknown for a mechanic to doze gently on the back seat as the bunch rolls dolefully through the sunflower fields of deepest France.

1400

When a rider punctures in the bunch he puts up his hand and also alerts his team car via the two-way radio in his racing top. The raised arm is usually seen by the red car directly behind the peloton. This is where the race director sits and it is the most important official car in the race. In this car is a very experienced driver, a multi-lingual Tour radio announcer, the race director and often a VIP guest.

All the announcements on Radio Tour are made from here, including any incidents in the peloton from punctures to crashes, and details of the race itself including time gaps to riders ahead and behind. Radio Tour will also warn the convoy of hazardous roads ahead and can be quite strident in its instructions to any vehicle not obeying its commands. When a rider signals that he has a puncture, the radio will announce the team name first, then the issue, a puncture and sometimes whether it is the front or rear wheel.

At the same time or even before the announcement is made on Radio Tour, the team car will have heard from the rider what the issue is over the team's internal closed radio system. Immediately the team car pulls out from its allocated position in the line of 22 cars. This is based on the team's highest rider in the general classification at the start of the stage. If it's in the second half of the 22 and the roads are winding or congested with riders behind the bunch, it can take minutes to reach the rider with a puncture.

In all continental pro bike races the team cars drive on the right hand side behind the bunch, the cyclists take the centre of the road and the motorcycles stay on the left. Team cars drive up to the bunch on the left hand side and it takes a skilled sports director at the wheel to pass cyclists, other team cars and motorbikes in the tight corridor behind the bunch.

These strictly observed rules of the road become clear when a rider has to stop for an issue like a puncture. When the team gets to the back of the bunch where the punctured rider is hopefully still riding on the soft or flat tyre (possible on tubular tyres) the sports director alerts the rider with his klaxon and both rider and car stop as quickly and as close together as possible.

The mechanic sits on the right side and jumps out either with a spare wheel or ready to grab a complete bike or spare wheel from the roof rack. Unless it's a serious emergency team cars always stop on the right hand side of the road.

All the team car racks are custom made and cost thousands of euros. They secure the bikes with single clamps which are easy and quick to operate. The wheels are secured by their quick-releases to vertical forks.

The mechanic's door opens safely in the right hand verge and the other team cars normally swerve around the stationary team car. Normally, the mechanic will know which wheel is punctured and if it is a rear wheel the rider will have put the chain on the smallest sprocket to ease its removal. If it's the front wheel the rider may have removed it but either way the cyclist holds up the bike while the mechanic releases the wheel and inserts a fresh one.

This process has become a more stressful experience for mechanics in recent times as they have had to contend with disc wheels, through axles and safety flanges which all add precious time compared to a traditional quick-release system with caliper brakes.

A team leader may get a complete bike if the puncture comes at a time when the bunch is racing hard. It is quicker to take a machine from the roof rack than replace a single wheel. The mechanic has a schematic of the bikes on the roof taped to the headrest in front of him and will know which side the rider's spare bike is located when he jumps from the car.

◄ When a star has a problem, a teammate will wait while the mechanic tries to fix it from the car.

Bikes loaded on team
car roof rack.

Every bike on the roof is also in the big ring on a big sprocket like the 19 so that the rider can accelerate quickly from a standstill and a push from the mechanic. In seconds the mechanic can have the rider on the new bike and with a running shove can ensure he returns to the bunch with a minimal effort, using shelter from the other team cars. As long as a rider is within the convoy there is a chance he can get back to the bunch after a puncture or mechanical issue.

1500

'Chute au peloton!' If there is one phrase guaranteed to jerk every mechanic into life it's the urgent announcement from Radio Tour of a crash in the peloton. Of all the multifarious duties of a pro team mechanic, the ability to stay calm but react to the rapidly unfolding scene of a big crash in the bunch is the most stressful part of his day.

When a crash is called over the radio, if it involves a dozen or more riders the whole convoy behind the race slams on the brakes and it can take a few seconds before Radio Tour begins to identify teams involved. In that time the crashed riders may have informed the team over the radio but either way mechanics will already be running up the stationary line of team cars carrying spare wheels and bikes.

If the rider is not injured, the mechanic must make a quick assessment of the damage and either use the spares he has carried up from the car or call for additional bikes or wheels which by now

the sports director might have brought up. In the chaos of a mass pile-up it can be hard to pick out the riders to help first, priority going to team leaders who may also take a wheel or even a bike from another crashed or stopped team-mate. There is not much time or the material to make repairs but a mechanic will straighten brake levers and check bars and wheels for damage using a hex key or a bit of muscle to temporarily bend something back in place.

Getting the riders back on the road is the priority and the work continues when the convoy is moving again, this time at high speed catching up and trying to pass riders chasing back to the peloton. Coming up alongside their team riders caught up in a crash the mechanic will double check the bike is functioning and either make an adjustment on the move or stop again to replace a wheel or complete bike.

1600

When it's hot, as it often is in July during the Tour, there is an almost constant circulation of team cars going up the line to pass up drinking bottles to riders, whose job it is to load up with drinks and hand them out to other members of the team. The mechanic's job is to retrieve bottles from the cooler next to him and pass them forward, up to a dozen at a time, to the sports director who then hands them through his open window on the left hand side to the rider. That is the other reason why the team cars drive on the right hand side because it places the sports director on the left where he can talk to and pass things to his riders in the centre of the road.

Mechanics may also be tasked with loading around five bottles into the special vests worn by riders who drop back for refuelling. The vest is passed through the window and put on by the rider as he pedals along. When he later rides up alongside a team-mate, he can simply pull a bottle from the back of the vest to hand over.

On the back seat next to the mechanic are side pockets filled with energy gels and stockings into which ice is packed for extra cooling on very hot days. The ice packs are passed to riders who place them under their jerseys just below the neck.

1700

Towards the end of a flat stage, Radio Tour will announce that the team cars are not allowed to drive up to the back of the bunch and pass food or drink to their riders. They have plenty of warning as the feeding cut-off point is announced at the

beginning of the stage. Usually it is close enough to the finish to ensure that the riders are all sufficiently supplied with fuel.

In the final hour, the speed invariably goes up and the increased risk of crashes and punctures means it's imperative to leave the rear of the bunch as free as possible from team cars not engaged in essential jobs. Not only that, at speeds well in excess of 60kph (37mph) it becomes too dangerous to have riders coming back for bottles or trying to avoid team cars as they chase behind the bunch.

While the action heats up in the bunch there is often a few moments of relaxation for the mechanics nestled in each team car. As long as there are no punctures or crashes, not a given by any means, all goes quiet in the team car as its passengers follow the race on screens and listen to the commentary on Radio Tour. If there is a puncture in a fast finale the team car

▲ One of the mechanic's many tasks is to hand up ice bags to riders from the team car.

◄ Riders and mechanics are in constant contact throughout the day.

▲ If a rider punctures late in the stage there is not a second to lose.

and mechanic will drive, jump from the car and change the bike faster than at any other time in the day. Everyone at the Tour, especially the mechanics, knows that just when all is calm and predictable, all hell could be about to break loose.

Just before the finish line the team cars are diverted off the course and follow a closed route around the line to a road or car park where the team buses are stationed. Riders cross the line and are greeted by team carers with drinks and towels and weighed down with rucksacks filled with warm clothing. If they are not required for the podium, they pedal slowly through the crowds to the team bus, leaving their bikes with the two mechanics. This is beyond the finish zone barriers, a hundred metres or so after the line, and the mechanics begin loading up the bikes onto roof racks.

At this point all everyone on the team wants to do is get back to the hotel, and as soon as the bikes are loaded the team car or van is driven away from the race and goes directly to the hotel. If there are riders on the podium a team car may have to wait behind to bring them to the hotel while the bus and another team car goes on ahead.

1800–2200 HOURS

On arrival at the hotel the team cars park up in an area set aside for the team truck and other vehicles. The bikes and spares are all taken off the roof racks and placed in small stands ready for washing. If all eight riders are in the race that's 16 complete machines plus two or more spare wheels. With all four mechanics reunited after their team and truck driving duties of the day, the after-race washing and servicing of the bikes can be shared out in the evening shift.

If it has been a dry day on normal roads,

▶ Team cars are diverted around the stage finish to an assembly point beyond the line.

the spare bikes and wheels which have not been used are not always washed and may just be quickly checked and the chains wiped and oiled, before going directly into the truck ready for the following day. If it has been raining or the roads have been very dusty, the spares will all be washed whether they have been used or not.

While two mechanics – often the two who have not been in the team cars that day – take on the washing and drying of the bikes, the other two begin work on the clean bikes, checking nothing has come loose or been damaged and then replacing any consumables like brake pads, chains and bar tape. If the following day's stage is in the mountains they may be kept busy replacing chainrings and cassettes and might even swap out derailleurs if very low gears are requested by the riders.

How the mechanics share out duties in the team car and truck depends on the team but some will elect to do blocks of stages in the team car followed by days with the bucket and sponge. Other teams may have one mechanic washing bikes for the whole race while the other three share out the rider's bikes between them, with each mechanic working on the same two or three bikes for the whole race. This makes it easier for them to stay on top of their rider's set-up and personal preferences, with much less chance of mixing up one rider's instructions with another.

Bikes involved in crashes are assessed for the seriousness of damage and parts are either replaced or the complete bike is changed for a spare, which may also require some building up with parts. Each rider on the team can have two or three road bikes and up to two time trial machines. That's around 30–40 bikes for an eight-man team at the Tour de France.

There are also up to 120 pairs of wheels to choose from with different carbon rim depths, which the riders will specify depending on the stage and wind conditions expected the following day. While the mechanics work on the bikes, the fans drift away to their evening meals while the riders have their massages in their rooms before eating. One or two may wander out into the hotel car park to discuss an issue with a mechanic or request something is changed on the bike.

At some point, preferably before nightfall but not always, the mechanics will break to eat in an area set aside for the team personnel. They may even have a well-earned cold beer and discuss the prospects for the next day, when the whole process starts over.

▼ Some riders make regular adjustments and changes to their bikes. They are well known to the mechanics!

No mechanic is ever seen without his trusty bike stand, which holds the bike securely at a convenient height.

CHAPTER 7:

JIGS AND TOOLS

Bikes are simple machines compared with other modes of transport. They are relatively easy to maintain and adjust with a few regular tools. In a well-equipped workshop and in the team truck of every pro team are drawers full of specialist tools, which may only be used occasionally but are essential in preparing and repairing race bikes. There is another set of even more bike specific tools and jigs which pro team mechanics rely on when setting up bikes to fit every rider on the team.

BIKE STAND

At any time during the Tour de France, the interested observer of team mechanics working in hotel car parks will see them attaching strange-looking jigs with long arms and sliding pieces to bikes. Referring to well-thumbed notebooks, or increasingly laptop screens, composed of figures and angles, they make tiny adjustments to the bike's saddle, seatpost and handlebars. The jigs they use to set up multiple machines for each rider look homemade and some of them are, although it is possible to buy some specialist bike set-up jigs. The jigs are essential tools for a busy pro mechanic because they allow him to do one of the most precise and important jobs on a bike many times over with absolute consistency.

These jigs are really only of use to a pro mechanic – to set up a bike at home you can do just about everything with a tape measure. It may take a bit longer but if you only have one or two bikes the need to make adjustments is far less frequent.

One of the biggest tools that a pro mechanic relies on totally and which is also well worth adding to the home mechanic's workshop is a bike stand. The main advantage of a bike stand is that it lifts the machine off the ground and can be adjusted so that whatever job the mechanic is working on he or she can do it standing upright and not doubled-over or on bent knees. You may not have dozens of bikes to wash, check and maintain every day for three weeks but if you did, the priority would be to make each job as physically stress-free as possible.

That is why you will see the mechanics using extra large buckets of soapy water on small trolleys with wheels to allow them to wash multiple bikes and wheel the bucket around without having to lift it. The same goes for bike stands – the bike is at waist height while the tools are also racked or placed on worktops close to hand. It's fatiguing and annoying to have to bend down or make an awkward stretch to reach a component and a tired and grumpy mechanic is more likely to make a mistake than a fresh one, literally on top of his bike and tools.

Bike stands come in different styles but the best ones use quality clamps and materials and have very stable fold out legs. Some hold the machine securely with a big clamp on the top tube or seatpost, though care must be taken not to overtighten the clamp especially on carbon frames. Unusual shaped top tubes can also pose issues for the clamps on this type of stand. An advantage of this type is that the complete bike can be held in the stand.

The other popular style requires the removal of the front wheel. The fork is clamped to the stand while the bottom bracket sits in a channel above the central post. This type of stand secures the bike in two places and is very stable, especially if the mechanic needs to use tools to work on the bottom bracket. A bike stand is also a great way to wash the bike, for the same reasons that pro mechanics use them – it elevates the machine and if the wheels are taken out it allows access to areas of the frame, which can be hard to reach if the bike is washed on the ground with the wheels in.

▲ A popular bike stand with clamp for front forks and foldout legs with a wide footprint.

▶ Saddle position on a time trial bike is critical and layback and angle are regulated by the governing body. A foldout ruler helps the mechanic get the nose at the correct setting.

JIGS AND TOOLS
COMPRESSORS

Tour team trucks also have jet washers and compressors sometimes powered with small generators if power from the hotel is maxed out. Does the home mechanic need these? Not really. A jet wash will blast away dirt and rinse the frame and wheels in seconds but it can also drive water into bearings, which can seriously shorten their working life. On a pro team that may not be such an issue as they will have replacement bearings to hand and to some extent will treat them as consumables which are replaced as a matter of course.

It is possible to use a jet wash carefully and avoid the bearings in the wheels, bottom bracket and headset, and if you watch pro mechanics they are also careful not to direct the nozzle of the jet directly at any bearings. But if you do not have a jet washer, a garden hose has enough pressure to shift grime from the bike, especially if it has been covered with a dirt-shifting spray beforehand. It won't blast the grease from your bearings either, but it's still advisable not to direct any jet of water directly at wheel bearings.

A compressor is essential for power tools and pumping up tyres by the dozen. Pro mechanics may rely on compressor power for a few jobs but for general bike maintenance there is no need for the home mechanic to use power tools. On the Tour the mechanics do not just work on the bicycles, they can also be expected to change wheels on team cars and fix any items of kit like the roof racks, and a compressor could be useful for heavy duty fixes.

A hand-held drill-style pump powered with a battery is also very useful at the race starts where the mechanic can double-check tyre pressures and top them up if necessary.

◄◄ In July it is often warm and light enough to work into the evening outdoors.

◄ A powerful jet wash in yellow powers the mechanics' power hose.

JIGS AND TOOLS

JIGS AND TOOLS

▲ Not for dentistry, these picks are used to fish out fiddly cables and wires.

TAPS AND DIES

A bare frame must be prepared before the main bearings in the headset and bottom bracket can be fitted. If the frame has threaded inserts they often need to be cleaned of old grease or paint so that the bearing cups can be screwed safely and fully in without damaging either.

On a newly painted frame there is always some paint on the threads and also on the face of the bottom bracket shell or headset. The paint should be removed down to bare metal at both ends of the bottom bracket and headset, not only to allow the bearing cups to seat correctly but also to square up both ends to ensure the axle and steerer are perfectly aligned.

These precision tools for cleaning and squaring up bearing cups are some of the most expensive and infrequently used items in the mechanic's workshop. For this reason it's worth asking a professional mechanic to replace a headset or bottom bracket, components which can last years before wearing out.

For more modern press-fit style bottom brackets and headsets the specialist tools for their removal and fitting are also precision-made and, to make matters more complicated, must be compatible with numerous bearing sizes across component and bike brands.

INTERNAL FISHING KIT

Internally routed cables and wires are commonplace on carbon fibre racing frames and the increasing integration of electronic components has added a dextrous skill to the pro mechanic's inventory. Fishing out cables and dropped items from inside a hollow carbon frame has become an infuriating but necessary part of installing and maintaining a modern bike's systems. There are not many off-the-shelf tools which make up the 'fishing kit' but telescopic magnets are useful for retrieving dropped steel fixings and various hooks and bent wires can be fashioned to pull through cables.

DERAILLEUR ALIGNMENT TOOL

If the gears are not changing as smoothly as they should, and if adjustment has already been attempted using the barrel adjuster on the rear derailleur, the rear gear could be bent or out of alignment. On electric gears it is even more important that the derailleur is correctly aligned with the cassette, as this will allow the auto-adjust function to work perfectly. These gear related issues are not uncommon on carbon frames with replaceable gear hangers as the frame or hanger, or both, are not always perfectly aligned.

A gear hanger can also be bent quite easily if the bike falls on the rear derailleur or is damaged in transit. That is why it is always worth unscrewing the rear derailleur when the bike is being transported in a bike bag. A misaligned gear hanger will not sit directly below each selected sprocket and can usually be diagnosed by looking directly behind the jockey arm to see if the jockey or pulley wheels sit directly below the selected sprocket.

It can be hard to detect a small offset in the hanger and the only way to check it properly is with a derailleur alignment tool. With the derailleur out and the back wheel in, the tool screws into the hanger. As long as the wheel is true, the end of the bar should maintain its distance from the rim at half a dozen points. If it does not, the handle can be used to very gently bend the hanger back into place, or indicate whether a replacement hanger is required. It is not unusual for new carbon frame back ends to be misaligned and sometimes the only way to align the derailleur is to use the alignment tool to tweak it into place.

A. Derailleur alignment tool

B. Tap and dies various

C. Bearing press tool

D. Tap and die

SET-UP TOOLS

Pro mechanics at the Tour de France use elaborate custom-made jigs and tools to set each bike up for the eight riders on the team. With multiple bikes per rider and no room for error they go for failsafe methods which guarantee a consistent result every time. The home mechanic also wants to ensure that his or her bikes are set up to their own bike-fit measurements but this can be done with less specialist tools than the pros.

Apart from the trusty tape measure, which can be used for the basics of seat height and reach to the handlebars, two useful additions are a digital spirit level and a plum line. The spirit level does not have to be digital but if you have your saddle at a slight angle, for instance, a note of the degree of lift or drop can guarantee it can be replicated across different bikes and saddles. A traditional plum line is the accepted method for determining the position of the knee over the pedal when it is at the maximum power position, pointing forward and parallel to the ground.

▲ A digital spirit level for saddle adjustment.

▶ A jig with adjustable base stand for setting saddle height and seat angle, which can also be used to measure how far the seat is behind the bottom bracket.

A. Digital spirit level

B. Traditional plumb line

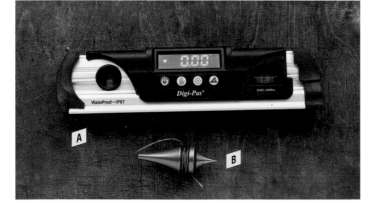

Every bike that has been ridden, and even some that have not but may have become dirty in transit, is washed after the stage.

CHAPTER 8:

BIKE WASHING AND AFTERCARE

Washing the grit and oil off a bike after a stage of the Tour is one of the most important daily tasks of the Tour de France mechanic. Cleaning the bike, drying it off, polishing and then lubricating it not only returns the machine to its stunning best, it prolongs the life of the components and gives the mechanics a chance to make initial checks for wear, damage or other issues.

BIKE WASH SET-UP

▲ Only after the bikes are washed and dried thoroughly are they worked on by mechanics doing checks and lubricating parts.

Watching a Tour de France mechanic washing a bike is the source of endless fascination for bike fans, usually gathered a safe distance from the jet washer. Most often located in a hotel car park, next to the tailgate of the team truck, the bikes are washed as soon as they are returned from the stage finish. Even if it's been dry and sunny on perfect roads, all eight machines and some or all of the eight rooftop spare bikes are washed every day regardless of how clean they look. There will always be oil to wash from the chain and drivetrain components, brake dust on the wheels and calipers and grime off the handlebars and top tube. The tyres, not just the sidewalls but equally importantly the treads themselves, must be scrubbed clean of any contaminants so that they can be checked later for wear or damage.

Not surprisingly, the mechanics on a team have got bike washing down to a fine art and mostly operate a rolling system in which one mechanic does the degrease, soaping and rinsing before handing the bike over to another who dries, lubes and polishes the bike. It takes only a few minutes for the first part, which is the most important and is the basic wash that a regular cyclist should perform at least every other ride. Time may be less of an issue for the regular cyclist, but the numerous simple yet time and effort-saving tricks of the pros should be worth considering.

BIKE WASH SET-UP

For degreasing and washing, the two things which make the job easier and effective are accessibility and kit. A Tour mechanic working on multiple bikes needs to have all his wash kit close to hand with the bike at waist level with the wheels out. For the amateur this holds true as it speeds up the job and also reduces back and knee bending efforts. Top of the list of kit for bike washing is a bike stand on which the bike can be worked on at waist height. Removing the wheels allows access to hard to reach areas primarily under the brake calipers and behind the chainrings, especially in the tight space in between where the rings are bolted to the chainset spider arms. It is also much easier to wash the wheels and tyres and degrease the cassette when they are out of the bike. Another back-saving tip is to put degreaser into an old bike bottle with the top cut off and to place it in the bottle cage where the degreaser brush can sit.

Pro mechanics will also have the jet wash next to the bike and may even have a large soap bucket on a low trolley base. Why risk tweaking your back lugging around heavy buckets of water, you are washing a bike not performing a core workout.

WASHING KIT

Bike stand
Cut down bottle
Low trolley or bucket stand
Jet wash or hose to hand
Wellington boots, overalls, rubber gloves

WASHING AND DEGREASING

The kit to wash a bike is inexpensive and with numerous bike tool brands now offering specialist brushes and sponges, easy to assemble. One of the most important tools is the degreasing brush, which can either be a bike-specific version or a standard or cut-down paint brush. Many pro mechanics favour a round-headed 'chalk' paint brush with fairly stiff bristles, wide and long enough to get right down between about two thirds of a cassette. This brush is used to put degreaser on the cassette, chain and around the chainrings. It can also be used on the derailleurs and under the brake calipers. Another essential accessory for degreasing the chain and keeping it in place is a chain keeper that screws into the derailleur-side dropout and allows the chain to run freely over it when the pedals are turned.

Tour mechanics use jet washers to clean off the degreaser and wash off soapy water. There are mixed views on whether this is advisable because a jet washer can force grease from bearings if aimed directly at them. Most pro team mechanics, however, use jet washes on low power and with a spray nozzle which they operate in a sweeping motion and do not hold directly over bearings. This should not drive grease from the wheel, bottom bracket and headset bearings, while the extra power to hand is better than a garden hose at cleaning off stubborn grime on wheel rims and tyres.

Finally, you need a big bucket of soapy water, preferably using bike or automotive shampoo, plus two sponges and a long handled bottle brush for the hubs and under the brakes. One sponge is for running the chain through after the degreaser has been washed off. The other is for the rest of the non-oily parts of the bike and wheels. Various size brushes for scrubbing the cassette and reaching nooks and crannies can be useful but you won't see pro mechanics using them very often because their machines never need that level of deep cleaning. Clean your bike regularly and it will not need the type of scraping tools required to clean the parts of a neglected machine.

WASHING AND DEGREASING KIT

Round-headed degreaser brush
Hose or jet wash
Big bucket
Two sponges
Long handled bottle brush
Bike shampoo
Bike degreaser
Assorted bike brushes and scrapers (optional)

◀ A cut-down cycling bottle makes a handy container for degreaser and brush applicator.

WASHING AND DEGREASING

1 Secure bike on stand with rear wheel still in. Position the bike with the chainset at waist height, adjusted to allow the bike to be turned freely through 360 degrees so you can stand in one place and access both sides by just swinging the machine around.

2 Turning the pedals backwards, apply degreaser and with the round-headed brush work it in along the outside of the chain on the big ring. Brush degreaser onto the outer edge of the big chainring as well. Work the brush into the back of the chain and chainrings, paying attention to the tight space where the rings are bolted to the spider. Move the chain onto another ring to expose the inner and outer teeth of all the rings.

3 Keep turning the pedals backwards and push the bristles into the cassette, working them in between the sprockets and moving the chain to reach every sprocket. Make sure any debris between the sprockets and hardened oil deposits are removed. Apply degreaser to the derailleurs, the derailleur jockey wheels and under the brakes.

4 Rinse off the degreaser with water from a jet wash or hose, making sure to use plenty of water on the chain and the cassette. Angle the nozzle from above rather than the sides to protect the bearings. Turn the pedals backwards as you spray the chain, chainrings and cassette.

5 Wrap the wet chain sponge into a fist around the chain and run the chain tightly through it for several revolutions. The chain, cassettes and chainrings should look like new after degreasing.

6 Remove the rear wheel and spray the bike with clean water from top to bottom, washing off as much of the loose dirt as possible. This will prevent abrading the frame when you sponge it down.

7 With the clean sponge and using plenty of hot water with bike shampoo from the bucket, wash down the bike starting from the saddle and working your way down. Lift the frame in order to access the underside of the bottom bracket shell.

TOUR TIP

Regular washing and lubing is the only way to maintain an as-new look for your bike. The less dirt you have to wash off the easier and quicker it is to keep your bike looking pristine. Washing a clean bike is a lot easier than one encrusted with dirt and old oil.

8 Be sure to clean under the saddle, inside the forks right up to and under the front brakes, on the inside of the chainstays and the seat tube below the front derailleur. Use the sponge and the bottle brush to get to tight spaces around the brakes and gears. Wash the derailleurs and pedals.

▶ It's easier to wash and check wheels when they are out of the bike. Don't forget to scrub the tyres!

9 Check there are no hardened deposits on the insides of the jockey wheels. Use degreaser or scrape them off. If the sponge is not oily, scrub the bar tape. Use a soft brush to clean the tape if it's very grimy.

10 With the clean sponge, and using plenty of soapy water, wash down the rims, spokes and hubs on the loose wheels. Use the long-handled bottle brush on the hubs if you can't get the sponge in. Hold the soapy sponge tightly over the tyre and rotate the wheel through it. Spray off the wheels with clean water.

DRYING, LUBING AND POLISHING SET-UP

Once the bike is clean and the now shiny sprockets, chainrings and chain are completely free from any trace of oil, the second part of the process can begin. This might be done by the mechanic who has washed the bike or, if the four mechanics are working a conveyor system, the bike will be passed on to another mechanic in an area less awash with running water and flying soap suds. The machine might initially be removed from the bike stand used for washing and carefully upended without its wheels, resting on its front fork and brake levers. When the second mechanic is ready he will collect the machine, secure it to his own bike stand

and begin the drying process. On-board compressors have made drying bikes with air hoses a common sight and they are very effective at driving out water around any moving or sealed parts, mechanical and electrical. Oil-free cloths and towels might also be used to wipe down the bike and thoroughly dry the frame and wheels.

DRYING, LUBING AND POLISHING KIT
Air hose
Micro cloths/towels/rags
Silicone/polishing spray
Aerosol water dispersant lube
Liquid chain lube wet/dry
Grease

THE IMPORTANCE OF A CLEAN AND POLISHED BIKE
Modern bikes will perform faultlessly in all weathers but they are also a lot more sophisticated than machines of old. Even a small amount of water in the wrong place can damage components like the recessed sealed bearings used in headsets, bottom brackets and wheels. Often overlooked are the bearings in both jockey wheels on the rear derailleur hanger and even the pivots in brake calipers and in both derailleurs. Moisture ingress can over time break down grease and oil and cause corrosion, destroying bearings and impairing the function of other components. Electronic components from derailleurs to computers and power meters are also universal on bikes used at the Tour.

Cables and connections are particularly susceptible to corrosion and potential

▼ An air hose is used to drive water from delicate components.

shorting from moisture ingress. These components are sealed and weatherproofed but they are of necessarily lightweight construction and when even the smallest fault can derail a rider's Tour de France, nothing can be left to chance when it comes to washing and drying a Tour bike. It might look like a purely cosmetic operation. It is a lot more important than that when a stage win or more is the price paid for a minor malfunction.

Polishing the bike is mainly for the looks. The Tour de France is marketing gold for the bike and component brands associated with the 22 teams and every day the mechanics spend time bringing every machine back to its immaculate best. When the fans descend on the team buses and cars before each stage they are there to see the bikes as much as the riders. Lined up in front of the team buses, the eight glittering bikes are inspected minutely from behind the pop-up barriers as the mechanics fuss around them making last-minute checks. Polished bikes look stunning but there is another reason to keep a bike clean and shiny with polish as it also protects the paint or carbon and encourages dirt and grime to slide off easily when the bikes are washed.

Hopefully, the amount of time and care that Tour de France mechanics put into cleaning their team bikes is proof that far from being a trivial activity, it is probably the most important job of their day. That is because daily quality time on every bike is much more than an exercise in making them look pretty again.

Cleaning a bike is nothing like washing a car, which can sit outside the house for weeks or months on end without

▲ Use a rag behind the gears to stop oil spraying onto the wheel rim.

deteriorating mechanically. A quick soap down of the bodywork returns it to good looks and the performance is unaffected. Leave a bicycle unwashed and after only a few rides, the accumulated dirt and hardened oil will start to wear components, reducing their lifespan and increasing the chances of an unexpected failure. Cleaning the bike ensures it continues to run smoothly and with minimal wear. It also gives the mechanics a chance to make a daily inventory of any parts that may need adjusting or require further attention. This daily MOT on every bike is a vital job and with a bike's finely engineered and precision components, there will always be minor tweaks.

TOUR TIP Use a cut-down nozzle on the spray lube as it makes it a lot easier to direct the lube at the desired component.

DRYING, LUBING AND POLISHING

▲ Use an old towel or soft cloth to dry the frame thoroughly.

1 Run the air hose around the frame in the bike stand, concentrating on all the areas where water may not have dispersed. This would include all bolts, cable ports, brake caliper pivots, derailleurs, between the fork crown and bottom of the headset and bottom bracket. Also any computer or head unit mounts and any electrical connections to a power meter.

2 If you don't have an air hose, leave the bike to dry in the sun or a breeze and then use cloths to dry it off, doing your best to reach the areas above. On less accessible parts, a blast with the water dispersing oil in an aerosol can drive out moisture. Hold an oily rag behind the part and wipe it off around the immediate area.

3 Apply silicone spray polish to the frame and carbon components. Wipe to a shine with a clean soft cloth. Polish the inside of the fork and chainstays and bottle cages, especially if they are carbon fibre. On painted or steel frames wax polish can also be used to good effect.

4 With aerosol or wet lube in a bottle go through the machine applying a small amount to the brake caliper pivots, exposed brake cables and adjusters, derailleur pivots and to the jockey wheel bearings. Wipe away the excess oil with a rag.

5 Put the back wheel in and position the chain in the centre of the cassette. With lube for wet or dry conditions, hold the nozzle just in front of the rear derailleur hanger, very close to or just touching the inside of the chain and squeeze enough out to deposit a small blob of oil on each link. Start at the quick-link and turn the pedals slowly, ensuring oil goes onto every link. When the quick-link comes around you know you have lubed the whole chain.

6 If you are expecting a long ride in the rain it can be worth smearing grease on the outside of the chain to help seal in the lube. Put a small amount of water resistant grease between thumb and forefinger and run the chain through them a few times. Wipe off excess with a rag.

7 Dry the wheels with a towel or clean rag. Do not polish them or get lube near the braking surfaces either on the rim or disc rotor. Check the skewers and levers are not corroded and working smoothly. Apply a tiny amount of oil to the lever and inside to the cam surface. Wipe the skewer rod with an oily rag.

8 Inspect the tyres for general condition, paying special attention to anything embedded in the tread, typically flints and thorns. Carefully pick them out with a thin blade. A tiny amount of water in the hole will bubble if there is a hole in the tube.

9 If the hole is big enough to see the tube inside, then the tyre should be replaced. A quick fix is to put a dab of rubber cement into the hole. Check the tread and sidewalls for splits and cuts. Any bulging in the tyre or exposed tubes requires the tyre to be replaced.

10 Remove the bike from the stand and fit the front wheel, double-checking the tightness of the quick-release levers in both wheels. The levers should always be on the left hand side of the bike and not too tight. Put your fingers behind the frame or fork to pull the levers on, ideally with the front lever horizontal and the rear outside the seat stays between vertical and horizontal.

TOUR TIP

When transporting wheels in bags and boxes it is worth putting them in bike bags to protect their spokes and tyres. If the wheels are going on a plane, make sure to let half the air out to prevent the tubes bursting in the low pressure hold.

Many daily jobs of a Tour de France mechanic involve simple checks using a few basic tools.

CHAPTER 9:

TOUR DAILY MAINTENANCE JOBS

Once the bikes are washed and lubricated, mechanics run through a series of daily checks and adjustments. These jobs may not be all that complicated, but they are crucial to the smooth running and safety of bikes that have been ridden hard for 200km (124 miles) or so. Keeping on top of these jobs is a sure way to pick up and act on issues before they get out of hand.

BOLTS, BRAKES AND ADJUSTMENTS

After every stage of the Tour each of the 22 teams return to their respective hotels where the mechanics are waiting at the team trucks to unload the bikes and begin the daily ritual of washing, lubricating and checking them over. Up to 16 bikes, including the eight which the team started on and eight spares from the roof racks, some of which will very likely have been used, are lined up in bike stands ready for washing and drying by at least two mechanics. Once the bikes are dried, oiled and polished, the mechanical phase of the daily maintenance jobs can begin.

BOLTS, BRAKES AND ADJUSTMENTS

This starts with bolt checks and minor adjustments while the mechanic is drying and lubricating the bike. It makes sense to do this first as the whole cleaning and lubing process is very hands-on. An experienced mechanic will use this process to detect an odd feel or sound from the bike. The bike is also in a revolving stand and the mechanic is working methodically through the bike drying and oiling. It makes sense to simultaneously check the same components for tightness with a hex key.

Some mechanics use a bike-specific torque wrench which can be calibrated to loadings in single figures. A typical adjustable bike wrench might have a range of adjustment from 0–7Nm (0–5ft-lb) or

▲ Check the seat post has not moved or come loose.

▶ Tyre pressures are set according to road and weather conditions.

a fixed rating of about 5Nm (3½ft-lb). Automotive torque wrenches are calibrated for higher loadings and should only be used on certain bike parts like cassettes and disc brake lock rings.

Some Tour mechanics also go on feel, using a manual hex tool with three sizes arranged in a star pattern for ease of use. Hex sizes of 4, 5, and 6mm will cover most of the components during this daily check. Only experienced mechanics should use their sense of feel on bolts used to secure parts made from carbon fibre. Strong in tension, carbon components are fragile when compressed by a collar or clamp and can easily be damaged by even a small increase in pressure. Alloy parts are more robust but can still be damaged by a heavy hand on the hex key. Even alloy threads, either inserted in carbon parts or alloy, are more easily damaged than a steel fixing and are easily overtightened.

Working through the bike the Tour mechanic will check the tightness of bolts on the handlebars and stem, the brake calipers

and pads, seat clamp, and the bottle cages. Drivetrain bolts which are checked include the rear derailleur and chainring bolts. It's important to remember that bolts are checked, not automatically tightened, which could lead to damage if they have not come undone and are overtightened.

Having sprayed the barrel adjuster and exposed cable on the brakes the mechanic may also screw down the adjuster and undo the bolt which clamps the brake cable. Holding the caliper arms against the rims, the bolt is done up again and can then be fine tuned by screwing out the adjuster. If the brakes have worn during the stage this will return them to their adjustment at the start of the day.

Brake pads should be changed when the material has reached the wear indicator mark. A visual check is enough, particularly after wet stages on dirty roads, when brake wear can accelerate alarmingly. Tour team mechanics will have a drawer-full of brake pads and won't hesitate to change pads at the first sign of excessive wear. The pads slide into a cartridge or holder which is bolted to the caliper arm.

It must sit with the closed end facing forward and is secured with a tiny grub screw. The bolt used to secure the cartridge to the caliper sits on a dome-shaped nut which allows the pads to be aligned at the correct angle to the rim. This is also with the leading edge of the pad about 2mm higher than the trailing edge. Toeing the brakes makes them come on more progressively and without screeching.

▲ If the bike looks right, it probably is right!

1 Work through the bike with a hex key checking the smaller hex bolts typically in sizes 4, 5 and 6mm. For ease of use and peace of mind use an adjustable bike specific torque wrench or a pre-set torque tool, typically set at 5Nm (3½ ft-lb) and with three hex bits.

2 Bolts to check at these torque loadings are usually handlebars and stem, brake calipers, levers and pads, seat clamp, and the bottle cages. Check the chainring bolts and rear derailleur mounting bolt.

3 On caliper brakes and with the wheels in make sure the barrel adjuster is screwed right down, with no thread showing above the barrel.

4 Pull back the brake lever which should not come back more than a third of its travel before making contact with the rim. If it comes back more than a third the brake should be adjusted.

5 Hold the brake pads against the rim with your hand and undo the bolt which clamps the cable to the caliper arm, just until the cable can move under the clamp. Holding the brake pads lightly against the rim, do up the clamp bolt to a torque setting between 6–8Nm (4½–6ft-lb).

6 Pull the brake lever to feel the brake adjustment and check that the pads are not touching the rims.

7 If one side of the brake pad is touching the rim the first thing to double check is that the wheel is in straight. Release the quick-release and push the wheel firmly into the dropouts.

TOUR TIP

Use an alloy end cap to finish the exposed end of the cable as it protects the cable from fraying and looks neat. Use cable cutters to cut the exposed cable which should extend no more than about 40cm (15¾in) from the pinch bolt. Crimp the alloy end cap with pliers, once near the base and once in the middle.

8 If the pads are still touching on one side, holding both arms of the caliper apart, pull the touching side of the brake slightly away from the rim. If that doesn't work the alignment can also be adjusted in or out by screwing the grub screw on the top or sides of the caliper arm.

9 To change the brake pads make sure the brake quick-release is off, unscrew the pad and cartridge and take them out. Screw out the grub screw on the cartridge

until the pad is released and slide it from the cartridge. Slide in replacement pads and tighten the grub screw.

10 Loosely re-fit the cartridges in the caliper and, with the quick-release back on, align them flat to the rim by pulling the lever on. To toe the pads some mechanics slip a credit card under the trailing quarter of the pads and then tighten the cartridge with the brake lever pulled back.

TYRE CARE AND GEAR CHECKS

Before putting the rear wheel back in the bike the tyres on both wheels are wiped down with a clean rag or towel and then closely inspected for wear, embedded material and any signs of damage. Turning the wheel slowly in his hands the mechanic is mainly looking for small cuts which may still have a fleck of stone in them – these can damage the tyre or, by working themselves in, cause a puncture later.

Anything bigger than a pin-prick will normally result in the tyre being replaced. An enthusiast rider need not replace a tyre with a small cut in it but careful removal of anything embedded in the tyre is crucial.

With the wheel in the bike, still in the stand, the final task which brings the cleaning phase to an end is to wipe any excess oil off the chain and do a thorough run-through of the gears. Whether they are electronic or cable, every mechanic on all 22 teams in the Tour will check the gears on a bike being prepared for the following day's stage.

If there is one thing that frustrates riders and can result in a wasted effort, it's a machine which is fluffing its gears or cannot access all 11 or 12 sprockets, especially the smallest one. With one hand on the bars working the levers or buttons and the other turning the pedals rapidly,

the mechanic keeps an eagle eye and an ear attuned to the correct sounds, as he methodically clack-clack-clacks the chain up and down the cassette.

If there is any hesitation between gear changes or if the chain does not run smoothly on every sprocket it can be fine-tuned using the barrel adjuster on the back of a cable-operated rear derailleur. A pro team bike will rarely require adjustment to the throw of its rear derailleur, which determines the limits of travel on the biggest and smallest sprockets. Nor will the mechanics need to adjust the distance between the top jockey wheel and the sprockets.

More likely is that the cable needs changing and all mechanics should check that both gear cables are running smoothly and that there is no damage to the cable itself or the outer cable housing, especially the part which loops from the back of the chainstay into the rear derailleur. This end

▲ Always check the tyres, as even a slow puncture can be picked up while wheeling the bike around.

▼ Double check the quick-release is not too tight, or loose.

of the cable is particularly susceptible to dirty rainwater, robbing the gear change of snappy changes. It's essential to keep the inner cable clean and free from a build-up of dirt.

A pro mechanic will change the cable at the first sign of stiffness, or even as part of a routine service. Fresh cables transform the feel of a bike, literally making it feel like new again. Cable inners are not expensive and if there are persistent issues with the slickness of the gear changes or the lever feels unduly stiff, a cable change is the first place to begin to remedy the situation.

Most of these issues affect the rear derailleur more than the front, which has a shorter cable and is tasked with a simpler job of shifting the chain between two chainrings. Once the derailleur cage, the part which makes contact with the chain and derails it, is set at the correct orientation to the big chainring, the front gear changes should remain consistent for as long as those chainrings are in use. Changing the big chainring, however, will require a minor correction moving the derailleur either up or down with a hex key and re-setting the tension in the cable.

Cables come in two parts, a wound steel cable which runs inside a protective outer. Cables for gears are thinner than brake cables and on modern bikes are often routed outside the frame, unlike the wires of an electronic gear system. If the outer cable housing is in good condition it is not always necessary to replace the outer. The short loop of outer housing which goes into the rear derailleur is worth replacing, however, as this part is crucial for smooth gear change feel at the lever.

▶ Running through the gears is on the daily post-stage checklist.

1 Check the tyres on both wheels. Thoroughly dry each tyre with a clean towel or soft cloth. Slowly rotate the wheel while inspecting the tyre for any signs of damage. Look for small holes or cuts and anything embedded in them. Carefully pick out any stone, glass fragments or thorns. If the cut is less than a couple of millimetres it can be filled with rubber solution from a puncture repair kit. Anything bigger, especially if the inner tube can be seen, would require replacement on a Tour bike.

2 With the bike in the stand put the back wheel in. The chain should have been oiled after the washing process. Turn the pedals and run through the gears on the big and small chainrings. Make sure the chain changes into the biggest sprocket from the small ring and onto the smallest sprocket from the big ring. Working between the small and big rings work the gears back and forth especially in the middle of the block.

3 If the derailleur is correctly set up for throw at both ends of the cassette and the top jockey wheel is also correctly positioned below the sprockets, put it into top gear on the smallest sprocket in the big ring and check cable tension. There should be no slack in the cable to the rear derailleur, which should move as soon as the lever is pushed in.

▲ Tyres are pumped up and valves checked for condition.

TOUR TIP Specialist dry lube for bike chains is best applied from a bottle. Slowly rotate the chain to ensure each roller gets at least one blob of oil. Let the oil infiltrate the rollers for an hour or so then wipe the chain with an oily rag.

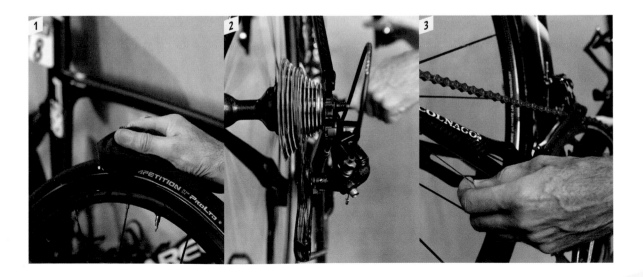

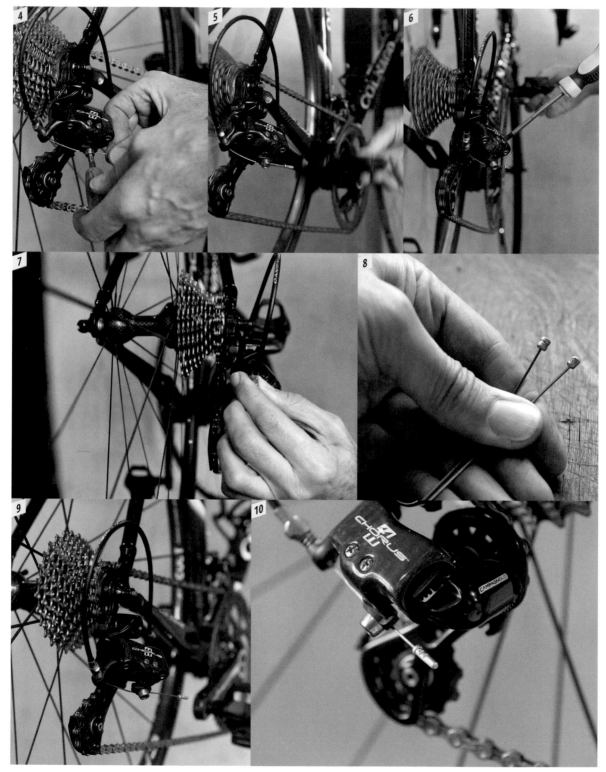

4 If there is some slack in the cable screw in the barrel adjuster on the rear derailleur and then back it out one full turn. Undo the bolt holding the cable, and with fingers or flat-nose pliers gripping the cable, pull it until it feels taught along its length. Do up the bolt with a hex key.

5 To check the gears are changing smoothly with or without altering the cable tension. With the chain in top gear on the smallest sprocket, visually check that both jockey wheels in the derailleur hanger are sitting directly in line below the sprocket. Click the gear lever once, changing up one gear.

6 If there is any hesitation in the change or if it goes into the sprocket but does not run smoothly, turn the barrel adjuster a quarter turn to move the derailleur a small amount either left or right. Clockwise for left or down the cassette, anti-clockwise for left or up the cassette.

7 When the gears are shifting efficiently between these two sprockets the derailleur should be in correct adjustment for all the sprockets, but check by running through all the gears and in both chainrings. It may be necessary to make another small adjustment in the centre of the cassette to get the gear changes spot on throughout all the gears.

8 To change a gear cable first you need to make sure you have the correct type of cable for your gear system. The best thing is to buy cables made by the same brand as your gears or aftermarket versions specifically for the same brand. It's very important to ensure the cable is the correct size and that the barrel-end fits the lever.

9 Check the condition of the outer cables, especially the loop which feeds the cable into the rear derailleur. If it's aged or there is evidence of encrusted dirt it is worth changing it. Make sure the ferrules fit snugly into cable stops and that the run of the cables from the levers follow the cleanest lines with no sharp bends.

10 Modern cables do not need oiling as they run in nylon-coated outers. Carefully feed the inner through the outer housings, securing the bare inner lightly with a hex key on the rear derailleur. Pull the cable until it is taught and tighten the bolt. Using cable cutters, cut the excess cable about 4cm (1½in) after the clamp and carefully crimp an alloy cable end cap to protect the bare end.

▲ Use a soft alloy end cap to prevent the end of the cable fraying.

TOUR TIP Only use cable cutters to cut bicycle cables, as their tightly wound construction will fray and come apart if the straight cutters on standard pliers are used. You may not use them very often but bicycle cable cutters are a toolbox essential.

During the stage, especially early on, mechanics are often called up to help a rider fix or adjust the radio used for communication.

CHAPTER 10:

DAILY ELECTRONIC AND DIGITAL JOBS

Electronics are everywhere on bikes ridden in the Tour de France. Gears are powered by on-board batteries, while power meters and head units display essential performance data. On most Tour machines, the brakes are the only components operated via a traditional cable, and as hydraulic disc brakes become more popular, bikes in future Tours could become entirely cable-free.

ELECTRONIC GEARS

You only have to look at the rows of power points which line the sides of Tour de France team trucks to know that one of the most important components of the modern bike is the rechargeable battery. Inconceivable not that long ago, the revolution in electronic functions has turned on its head the idea of the bike as a manually operated machine. The rider still has to push on the pedals, of course, but the way he controls and monitors his progress now has more in common with an in-flight computer than a bicycle.

▲ Battery powered SRAM Red eTap electronic front derailleur.

ELECTRONIC GEARS

The most eye-catching development in recent times has been the almost universal adoption of electronic gears. Electronic gears are not new, very little is in cycling,

and there were attempts by various manufacturers in the 1990s to create reliable electronic gears for both leisure riding and racing. But it took until 2009 for Japanese component giant Shimano to finally produce electronically powered front and rear derailleurs good enough for regular use in professional racing. In 2009, a few teams rode Shimano Dura-Ace Di2 gears in the Tour de France. Legendary Italian groupset brand Campagnolo followed soon after in 2011 with their own electronic gears system, EPS. Both the Shimano and Campagnolo versions used similar systems with a single battery operating gears powered by servo motors via wires routed through the frame. A small control box, fixed below the stem or increasingly fitted integrally in the frame or bar ends, displayed battery life and tuning functions.

In 2015 US brand SRAM introduced their innovative wireless gear shifters, eTap, which used front and rear derailleurs

A. Campagnolo EPS control unit

B. Campagnolo Record EPS front derailleur

C. Campagnolo Record EPS rear derailleur

D. Campagnolo band turns system off

operated remotely from the brake levers and powered with a small rechargeable battery in each derailleur. For a mechanic, eTap is the simplest groupset to fit as all they have to do is bolt on the front and rear derailleurs, attach the brake and control levers and the gears are ready to go. One of the most time consuming and fiddly jobs for the modern mechanic is preparing a machine for the installation of gears with wires and a remote rechargeable battery. They are used to fitting Shimano and Campagnolo systems and have got it down to a fine art, but if there are problems with the routing of the wires, or damage or corrosion affects their operation, the diagnosis and fix can be a time-consuming distraction.

Daily maintenance jobs for the Tour mechanic are to check that the gears are still in adjustment after the stage. They will give them a full run through after the bike has been washed and dried. Although there is an auto adjust function on electronic derailleurs they may still need to be re-calibrated if the wheel or cassette has been changed. This is a semi manual job with the control box set in the correct function allowing the gear mechanism to be micro tuned until it runs smoothly and quietly on the sprocket. After that the derailleur can be set to its regular changing function in which it will auto adjust on all the sprockets each time a gear is selected.

Battery charging is not necessarily a daily requirement and the many batteries in all the bikes may be charged only every few days or not at all if they have not been used, say in a spare bike. When the bikes are in transit and especially if they are ever transported in a bike bag, the systems are either switched off or disconnected, because if a button or lever is accidentally pressed or held down it can completely drain a battery and possibly damage a servo.

E. Shimano Di2 charge port on Pinarello

F. Shimano Dura-Ace Di2 front derailleur

G. Shimano Dura-Ace Di2 rear derailleur

NO MORE CABLES

Since the introduction of electronic gears it has taken just a few years for cable-operated gears to become virtually redundant in the Tour de France peloton. Some older riders preferred to use traditional gears for a year or two but such is the fast turnover in pro cycling, a generation of riders are already emerging having raced more of their careers on electronic gears than cable operated ones.

Commercial pressure has played its part. A professional rider is under contract to ride the brands associated with the team and if they are asked to trial a new component, they are often obliged to do so. But the enthusiasm with which pros have adopted electronics is in stark contrast to their caution over disc brakes. It would be true to say that electronic gears have been an innovation introduced from the top-down while disc brakes have achieved widespread acceptance at the grass-roots level which is now pushing a commercial imperative on professional teams to adopt them.

Professional cyclists like electronic gears because they have proved to be extremely accurate and reliable but more importantly, they make changing gear under load possible. They can also be operated by simply pressing on a button

▲ SRAM Red eTap levers showing gear change paddles.

sited anywhere on the bars. With a cable-operated gear, especially on the front changer, the rider has to finesse the gear change, often by reducing his force on the pedals while the chain is moving from one chainring or sprocket to another. A ham-fisted gear change can derail the chain and even damage teeth on the sprocket. One of the genuine advantages of electronic gears is how smoothly they move the chain between the sprockets and that is especially the case with the front changer which has been transformed when operated via a servo.

Another feature loved by the pros is the freedom to change gear using satellite shifters positioned anywhere on the handlebars. For sprinters that means they can change gear while sprinting at full power while riding out of the saddle on the drops. The little button to change gear is sited on the inside of the bar below the brake lever right where the thumb can reach it, while the hands are gripping the lower part of the bars.

Climbers may ask the mechanic to put a satellite shifter in the centre of the bars where they can change gear while riding hard on a mountain pass with their hands resting on the tops of the bars. In a high pressure situation on a climb a rider needs to be able to change gear with the minimum of effort. He may also value the fact that he can change gear without

TOUR TIP | When transporting bikes with electronic gears it is worth turning off or unplugging the derailleurs to ensure that they are not accidentally triggered during transit. A flat battery or worse, burned out derailleurs could result in an expensive fix.

moving his hands from the centre of the bars to the brake lever, which could signal to his rivals that he is either about to attack in a bigger gear, or is trying to hide his acute suffering by surreptitiously changing into a lower gear.

Where the gear buttons are placed were not an option on cable gears but now they are part of a rider's set-up which the Tour mechanic will have in his rider database. It may vary from bike to bike as well. As the weight of bikes with electronic gear systems has come down and are now comfortably at the minimum bike weight of 6.8kg (15lb), a reason for not fitting a satellite shifter would not be due to its additional weight.

There's another advantage to electronic gears never available to traditional derailleurs. Every gear system is programmable, often via an app on a phone or laptop, with an extensive range of gear shifting options available to the rider. This might simply be assigning front and rear mechanism to either brake lever or satellite button, or it could determine how many multiple shifts are performed when the button is held down. More sophisticated options could also include an automatic function which switches between the two chainrings and the sprockets if the gear selected has a more efficient chain line.

These are all jobs which a mechanic may be asked to program, or even may suggest to the rider, as updates are regular and may be presented to the team mechanics whenever necessary by roving technical staff of the component brands. In the off-season when the new bikes are being assembled, there are often new versions of the derailleurs and that is when all the mechanics can undergo some training on the new parts in seminars run by the manufacturers. And when there isn't a technical expert to hand the mechanic just does what everyone else does with modern electronics – goes online for advice on how to fix it!

▲ Satellite gear change buttons are fitted to time trial bars.

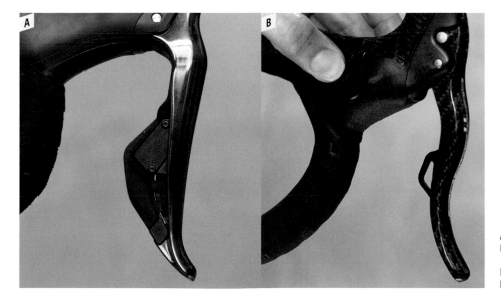

A. Shimano Dura-Ace Di2 lever

B. Campagnolo Record EPS lever

DAILY ELECTRONIC AND DIGITAL JOBS

POWER METERS

Every team and most riders have a power meter on their bikes. Fitted behind the chainset or in the pedal body, power meters use strain gauges to measure the power being exerted by the rider. They communicate the power in watts to a head unit fixed to a bracket which extends forward of the stem. There are numerous power meter brands and head units which can be paired and riders may use the team's power meter with another brand sponsor for the head unit, often Garmin. There is some controversy around riders using power meters to monitor their performance as some believe it results in less exciting racing. If every individual just rides to their maximum climbing power, for instance, the tactical element of a race will be lost, they argue.

Short of checking that the power meter unit is undamaged and all the connections are clean there is little that the Tour mechanics need to do other than recharge batteries. The head units are retained by the riders as they will be used to download information from the stage later for analysis. Some riders will also share their figures for a stage later in the day, which can provide an extra and fascinating insight into how the stage unfolded and the level of effort put it to achieve the result.

There's very little a modern head unit cannot tell the rider beyond just about every performance figure he needs, including the basics of power, speed, distance, time elapsed and so on. A head unit can display the cadence and the gear the rider is in, although it needs a separate sensor for this. It can also be used to display weather alerts and its GPS function can be used to display all the relevant information about the roads to be covered by the stage. If you include the radio pack which riders use to communicate with the team car behind the race, today's Tour rider is more connected than ever before.

▲ A typical head unit with a centrally mounted clamp.

▶ Power meter on left-hand crank.

COMMS AND TV

Team radios are another electronic device that need to be collected after each stage and charged in time for the following day. One of the most common tasks that the mechanic in the team car performs while alongside a rider, is to check the connections of a team radio and earpiece. The radio usually sits in a central pocket high up on the back of the jersey but the wires to the earpiece can sometimes need checking and the radio might be changed if it is faulty or has a flat battery.

In recent Tours there has been a revolution in information sharing from riders in the Tour as well the coverage itself, with the high quality TV coverage from the motorbikes and helicopters supplemented by on-board footage shot with miniature GoPro cameras attached to the bikes. These cameras are fitted by the mechanics with help from the camera technical team. These can be placed under the bars, near to the stem facing forward and also under the seat facing backwards. They add a small amount of weight but it's negligible. If anything, the extra drag of a forward mounted camera may put some riders off from agreeing to fit a camera, especially on a time trial machine. When used, these mini sports cameras have produced spectacular footage showing for the first time unique action and crashes from inside the peloton.

TOUR TIP For stages on rough roads and cobbles a small piece of electrical tape over the head unit bracket will hold it more securely in place and prevent it moving in its mounting point.

▲ The yellow jersey checks his radio is working during a stage.

◀ Mini sports cameras are attached below the bars and under the seat.

Mechanics are responsible for keeping team vehicles clean and shiny throughout the three-week race.

CHAPTER 11:

NON-BIKE AND REST DAY MAINTENANCE

If you thought there was no end to the jobs allotted to a pro mechanic at the Tour de France, the additional tasks of maintaining crash helmets, setting up shoes and washing the team cars, will not come as a surprise. If there is a spare moment in the day, the mechanics will fill it with one of these non-bike related jobs, which can be as crucial to the team's performance as almost any other.

HELMETS

The crash helmets of pro riders in the Tour have a tough life, and sometimes a short one as any helmet that sustains an impact in a crash is destroyed and directly replaced with a new one. A rider may use multiple helmets during the Tour, especially if the individual or team takes the lead in a classification, which gives the helmet brand a great opportunity to match their helmets to the colour of the jersey.

One of the most visual helmets is bright yellow, not just for the leader of the race, but for the team which leads the team classification. Traditionally this was indicated by the team wearing yellow racing caps but today the yellow helmet, provided by the team's helmet sponsor, is one the easiest things to spot in the bunch.

The Tour is also the biggest shop window of the year for new tech and helmet manufacturers are no different, taking advantage of all the media coverage to launch new models.

Long gone are the days when the helmet was seen as a necessary evil imposed on cyclists by racing governing bodies. Modern helmets are not only safer, lighter and more aerodynamic, they also look great and there is an endless choice of shapes and colourways. Every team at the Tour has a helmet partner which supplies the team with their top-of-the range helmets in team colours.

There could be several different helmet choices throughout the Tour as well, from standard lightweight road helmets with big vents for hot weather stages, to more aero road helmets favoured by sprinters and full aero helmets with extended teardrop shapes and integral visors.

There are spare helmets in the team car for every stage and it is not unusual to see a rider return to the team car and, while riding alongside the open window, change a helmet or make an adjustment with the help of the mechanic. Often it will be related to the straps which can chafe or may just need to be adjusted. Helmets are usually adjusted with a buckle on the strap, which can be fiddly to alter while wearing the helmet, and via a dial at the back that

▲ A team will bring dozens of helmets to a race like the Tour.

▶ Mechanics will help riders select and adjust or modify helmets.

▶▶ Long-tail aero time trial helmets cannot be used for road stages.

◄ Every helmet is in either team colours or is matched to one of the individual or team classifications.

can easily be turned and which adjusts the fit of the internal cradle.

CARE OF HELMETS

A bicycle crash helmet is made from an impact absorbing thick polystyrene foam moulding in various sizes, which is covered by a thin plastic protective shell. The helmet is secured with straps, adjusted with a buckle and inside the bowl there is a cradle which adjusts to the circumference of the wearer's head. Around the inside of the helmet are padded comfort strips which can often be removed or swapped out for thicker or thinner alternatives. A helmet that has been well looked after and not subject to duress in a crash need not be replaced for three years or more. Helmets should be stored away from direct sunlight in a well-ventilated area after use. To maintain the pads, straps and the looks of the outer shell, helmets should be washed periodically depending on usage and conditions.

At the Tour, helmets will be washed by a mechanic on the rest days with a sponge and big bucket of soapy water. Strong detergents higher or lower than 7pH should not be used as the materials can be sensitive to alkaline or acidic additives. Gentle soapy wash for kids is safe to use. Bicycle helmets should never be put in a washing machine or dishwasher and rinsing them with a jet washer is also not recommended as water ingress under the outer shell or in any joints can affect the integrity of the helmet.

Most helmets have detachable internal pads and these can be removed for washing. Also the cradle can sometimes be removed and washed separately. All drying should be done away from direct sunlight and in a well-ventilated area. Do not put helmets on a radiator or use a hair dryer as direct heat is not good for the polystyrene moulding. Make sure the helmet is completely dry before storing it in a helmet bag. The thin plastic outer shell should be washed gently and if there is a lot of grit on the surface and in the vents carefully rinse it away using your fingers or a soft brush.

SHOES

There are three contact points on a bicycle: where the rider sits on the saddle; holds the bars; and turns the pedals. Team mechanics are responsible for all three and will know, to the nearest millimetre and degree, the positions, angles and preferences of all eight riders on the team. Saddles and handlebars are relatively simple to set up. Pedals are easy too, with just the tension in the cleat retaining spring adjusted to suit the individual rider.

Shoes also need to be carefully set up with shoe plates in the preferred position on the sole. This is one of the most precise jobs that a mechanic performs as it determines the position of the shoe on the pedal and must exactly correspond to the rider's set-up data.

Setting up shoes is one of the jobs where you will often see the rider and mechanic working together. They will often use a custom-made jig, sometimes with captive pedals into which the shoe is engaged with the shoe plates loosely fitted. The plates can then be lined up against marked positions on the jig until they correspond to the rider's settings.

Riders will bring more than one pair of shoes to the Tour and it is essential that the shoe plates on all shoes worn during the race have shoe plates in identical positions. If a shoe plate is positioned incorrectly it could result in a knee injury which could finish a rider's Tour de France and develop into a career-threatening issue if it is not addressed.

There's a drawer in one of the team truck units full of shoe plates offering various degrees of lateral float as well as shims to go under the shoe plates. There may also be spares for various shoe brands, including the quick-release dial systems in widespread use. In a crash the shoes can easily be damaged but, if they can be repaired, the rider may prefer to keep a pair of shoes he knows are set-up correctly than risk a new pair.

And when you see a neat hole cut into the side of a Tour rider's shoe it may not have been damaged in a crash but modified by the rider with some help from the mechanic, to relieve some pressure. High temperatures and long stages in July can be very hard on even an experienced and battle-hardened cyclist.

Most shoe plates are fixed to the sole of a racing shoe with a three-bolt design that allows the plate to be positioned for every rider preference. On popular brands there is also a choice of shoe plates with various plastic tongues designed to either lock the foot in place or allow for some lateral movement. Riders can choose which they prefer and can also use thin shims under the plate to compensate for a difference in leg length. On the back of the pedal there is also a screw that determines the tension on the quick-release spring, something sprinters will often ensure is set to its tightest setting to prevent their feet coming out in the furious action of a sprint.

▲ Adjusting a shoe while hanging from the window of a moving team car is a delicate operation.

▶ Teams have custom-made jigs to get the position of shoe plates absolutely spot on.

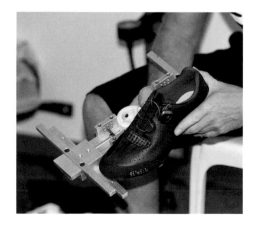

REST DAY JOBS

▲ There's a relaxed atmosphere around the team truck on a rest day but the work goes on!

There are two rest days during the three-week Tour de France but don't be deceived, there is no rest for the mechanics at any point during the race and that goes for the rest days, which can be busier than a normal stage. First, they often have to make a long drive to a hotel many hundreds of kilometres across France, as the rest days are often scheduled to coincide with a shift from one region to another. A long drive in a team car or truck the night after the previous stage might see the mechanics arrive at the rest day hotel in the small hours. Meanwhile, the cyclists will have flown and already be asleep in their rooms, back in their regular regime. If it's a very long transfer, say 500km (310 miles), the mechanics may drive half the distance the night after the stage and then complete the distance early the following morning.

In the morning the mechanics will be up at the usual early hour to prepare bikes for the traditional short rest day ride, which no rider misses as they need to keep their legs turning over. Setting off mid to late morning, it is a relaxed affair and sometimes local riders will tag along or corporate guests get to ride alongside their investments – if they are fit enough. They may even stop for a coffee.

The bikes are washed and checked after the ride just like a regular stage, and all the spare bikes are also washed. Mechanics will take the opportunity to double-check all the bikes are correctly set up, a painstaking job. All the chains on the road bikes that have been ridden will be changed. Each road bike will normally have two new chains during the Tour. Lots of new bar tape is also put on the bars of the road bikes. Bar tape lasts about a week on an average Tour but will be changed if it's scuffed or marked. It's also a good day to catch up on preparing, glueing and fitting tubular tyres to wheels. The rest day is a good day for catching up on those jobs that may have slipped down the list. It explains why Tour mechanics dryly refer to it as the day when the 'rest' of the work is done!

Helmets and shoes will also be washed and dried, and cyclists, after press conferences, will drift down from their rooms to discuss with the mechanics any issues with their bikes or equipment. Team cars and vehicles will have a thorough wash too. Interiors will be cleaned out and any small signs of damage tidied up. Team cars are well driven but in the many tight situations they find themselves in during a stage it is not unusual to sustain a bump and a scratch here and there. The rest day is one of the few opportunities the mechanics may have to take a team car to a garage for a new tyre or mechanical fix.

TOUR TIP

If you are fortunate enough to be invited to ride with a pro team on their rest day leg-stretching ride, you may get lucky if you ask one of the mechanics to help with a small adjustment to something like your gears or brakes.

The rear disc brake and rotor on a Tour bike shows latest through-axle system of securing the wheel in the frame.

CHAPTER 12:

DISC BRAKES ON PRO BIKES

Mountain bikes have had disc brakes for years but their take-up on road bikes has only just begun in significant numbers. Professional cycling has taken a cautious approach to disc brakes for a number of reasons but they are rapidly gaining acceptance. At the Tour de France, disc brakes are not an unusual sight and in 2017 a bike with disc brakes won its first-ever stage.

DISC BRAKES ON PRO BIKES

DISC BRAKES

Disc brakes were introduced to mountain bikes at the turn of the millennium and off-road cyclists were quick to recognise the performance and extra tyre clearance offered by hub-mounted discs. They appreciated the consistent power and clean running in muddy and wet conditions. An added bonus was the lack of wear on traditional rims, which not only lasted longer but could also be built without having to incorporate a braking track. As mountain biking became more focussed on extreme downhill courses and dual suspension machines overtook hard tails, disc brakes enabled mountain bikers to go faster, more safely.

Road bikes are not required to go flying down the sort of downhill courses which a mountain biker would take for granted. Nor are they expected to be used in conditions in which the wheels are sinking in mud. On a mountain bike the additional weight of disc brakes has also been a worthwhile trade-off against their power and precision when entering a tight bermed corner for instance.

For these reasons it has taken a lot longer for bike and component makers to produce a disc brake system for road bikes which meets the acceptance of racing cyclists.

But since the world governing body permitted limited testing of disc brakes in 2015, the weight of disc brake systems has come down while bike manufacturers have rushed to catch up with disc brake compatible frames and forks. Concerns over the safety of discs in the event of crashes have also been allayed. Discs or rotors now have chamfered edges and incidents of discs cutting riders involved in pile-ups have either been shown to be false or so rare as to be negligible. Lightweight plastic disc covers would solve the issue of exposed disc edges but it has not been deemed necessary to make them obligatory.

Another safety issue related to discs is the heat build-up in the disc during prolonged braking. This has led to concerns over riders and even mechanics suffering burn injuries in the event of a crash on a long descent or at any point when heavy braking has heated up the discs. Manufacturers have addressed these concerns with additional cut-outs in their discs designed to aid cooling and also by incorporating a layer of aluminium sandwiched between the steel braking surface of the disc. Aluminium conducts heat away from the braking surface. It's not just riders who would prefer not to put their hands onto a hot disc in the event of a pile-up, mechanics are also concerned about hot discs when handling crashed bikes and changing wheels.

The extra weight of earlier road bike hydraulic brake systems, about 500g (1lb), over conventional cable-operated caliper brakes has also been addressed, and there are now professional racing bikes with disc brakes which tip the scales at the minimum 6.8kg (15lb) weight limit. That is quite an achievement because it is not just the extra weight of the levers, hydraulic calipers and discs which have been pared down. The frame and forks, wheels and hubs, which all have to be modified and strengthened, have also had to be lightened to get the weight of a racing bike closer to the lightest machines with traditional caliper brakes.

▲ Disc brakes were first used on mountain bikes.

▶ Front rotor is bigger than rear, which needs less stopping power.

DISC BRAKE PROS AND CONS

On a road racing bike, disc brakes offer powerful and consistent braking in all conditions. In the rain especially, when braking on carbon rims can be grabby and unpredictable, disc brakes are virtually unaffected. A well set-up system can also offer a lot of feel, allowing the rider to get closer to the point before the wheels lock up. On long descents in the wet with heavy braking on corners a rider on disc brakes could gain valuable metres on every corner. If one rider on discs can outbrake another on caliper brakes on the final wet corner of a stage, that could be the difference between winning and losing that day. It remains a concern, however, that in a peloton of cyclists, some on discs and others on traditional caliper brakes, that there could be serious safety issues caused by the differential in stopping distances during hard braking in the rain.

While braking performance of discs over cable-operated caliper brakes may not be game changing in professional cycling, there has been a beneficial knock-on effect resulting in the removal of caliper brakes from the fork crown and seat stays. The extra clearance around the tyre has allowed the fitment of higher volume tyres which can run at lower pressures with no loss in rolling resistance. As a result tyres with a 25–26mm (1in) profile are now the default choice for the Tour peloton. Before, a 23mm (1in) tyre was the most

popular, but with tight clearances around traditional brakes, going any bigger was not always possible.

Fatter tyres not only offer more comfort and confidence-inspiring handling, their enlarged contact patch can also be exploited with harder braking on disc brakes. When a stage of the Tour includes sections of cobbles or gravel roads the mechanics can fit even fatter 27–30mm (1¼in) tyres on their disc equipped road bikes, adding versatility to the standard road machine.

These are the positives for disc brakes but there remain drawbacks. On aero race bikes a disc brake has been shown to be less aerodynamic than a traditional caliper brake. The golf ball-sized fork mounted caliper and the disc or rotor itself disrupt the airflow through the wheel. As aero advantages are highly sought after in virtually every aspect of road cycling, discs are a step back on the road to creating a super-aero bike.

Then there is the issue of brake pad rub, contaminated discs and braking noise. A quality disc caliper should not rub as the pads should be self-centring but that will not stop pros fretting that it does. Look at any pro when he takes his bike at the start of a stage and more often than not he will first inspect that the brakes are running freely. During a race some will even take off the quick-release just to make sure the brake is not rubbing. A disc brake may be set up to allow the disc to run freely between the pads but there is no guarantee that they will not go out of adjustment during the stage or that a replacement wheel will not rub on the disc.

▲ Rotors are drilled and slotted in order to help dissipate heat.

Which brings us to the most serious issue facing the adoption of disc brakes in races like the Tour de France. Compatibility between wheelsets and frames and the speed at which a wheel can be changed is taxing team mechanics and neutral service as they search for ways to return riders to the peloton as quickly as before. For team mechanics with a compatible disc wheel replacement it can still take precious extra seconds to put the fresh wheel in and line up the disc with the caliper, slotting into a gap of a few millimetres without knocking the pads off line.

If the bike has through-axles the change can take even longer, as the axle must be screwed into the frame, taking longer than a traditional quick-release lever. Faster through-axle closure systems are on the way but for the time being, when a fast wheel change is required at the Tour, team mechanics are playing safe and rather than fluff a wheel change they are grabbing a complete spare bike from the team car roof rack. That is less of an option for the neutral service car which has a limited number of bikes on the roof. But if caliper brakes remain popular, which looks very likely, they must carry both disc and wheels for traditional caliper brakes. As well as disc wheels for through-axle bikes and conventional quick-release. If you wondered why Mavic neutral service mechanics look stressed from time to time now you know why!

▲ Wheel changes on bikes with disc brakes is a new skill that mechanics must learn to perfect.

DISC BRAKE CHECKS AND MAINTENANCE

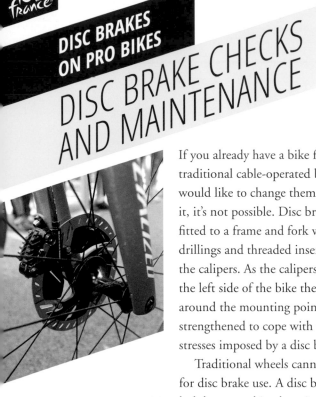

If you already have a bike fitted with traditional cable-operated brakes and would like to change them for discs, forget it, it's not possible. Disc brakes can only be fitted to a frame and fork with the correct drillings and threaded inserts to accept the calipers. As the calipers are fitted on the left side of the bike the frame material around the mounting points must also be strengthened to cope with the asymmetric stresses imposed by a disc brake.

Traditional wheels cannot be converted for disc brake use. A disc brake enabled hub has a machined carrier with drillings threaded to accept the disc or rotor. When pressure is applied to the disc it also exerts a powerful twisting stress on the spokes

and a wheel for disc brakes must also be built with stronger spoking patterns to withstand these stresses. This can also affect the way the wheel is attached to the frame, and many disc-braked bikes now have a through-axle style closed dropouts.

Many top road race bikes offer a choice between a traditional caliper model and a disc brake version. Quality disc brakes are hydraulic, with brake fluid contained in a sealed system which should only need periodical maintenance when the fluid is changed. Fluid changes should be made according to the manufacturer's schedule or before if they start to feel spongy at the lever. With a brake bleed kit, which drains and replaces fluid without allowing air to enter the system, the home mechanic can perform a fluid change but it's best to leave this job to a pro mechanic. A pro mechanic can also check if the discs are bent and

▲ Chamfered edges on the rotors have made them safer in the event of a pile-up.

▶ Mechanics working on disc brake machines at the Tour.

◄ Every major bike brand
now has a professional-
level racing bike with
disc brakes.

use an alignment tool to tweak them back into place.

Pad changes are much easier as most pads can be changed with a screwdriver and long nosed pliers to remove a split pin. Change the pads when they are worn to the edge of their wear marks, the same as you would with conventional pads. The only time you may have to change them before this is if they are contaminated with oil which has found its way onto the disc. Spraying the bike with oil is the easiest way to inadvertently put oil on the discs and it can be very hard to get it off. Hard braking can burn off some oil but if the discs and pads are already contaminated they lose feel and power. Use disc brake cleaner on the discs and lightly sand the pads.

When the pads are out check the condition of the pistons in the calipers and use brake cleaner to remove brake dust and any build-up of dirt. Use the lever to pump the pistons out a few millimetres but no more and make sure the pistons are shiny and not pitted or corroded. A small amount of oil on the sides of the pistons will help them go in and out.

If the pads are rubbing, the first thing to do is check that the wheel is in straight. If they are still rubbing loosen the caliper with a hex key and pull on the brake. With the lever pulled back hard, do up the bolts and the caliper should be centred on the disc again. On a flat mounted caliper it may be necessary to remove the wheel and replace it with something like a business card folded over the disc which pushes the pads back when the wheel is put back in. When the caliper is tightened it should align both the caliper and the pads away from the disc on both sides.

Replacing the sprockets from a cassette hub with fresh sprockets is a regular job for the Tour mechanic.

TOUR de FRANCE™

CHAPTER 13:

REPLACING WORN COMPONENTS

The home mechanic does not need a truck-full of tools to keep his bike in near perfect working order. Apart from the regular job of cleaning and lubricating the bike, there are a few components on the bike which should be regularly checked and if necessary, replaced. These are the bike's consumables, you should not expect them to go on forever and knowing when and how to change them will ensure your bike rides and looks like a pro rig.

BAR TAPE REPLACEMENT

1 Change the bar tape when it is damaged, worn, discoloured or you just want another colour! Remove the old tape, taking care not to leave too much broken tape and sticky residue on the bars. Clean the bars; if you want to get them completely free of old adhesive use isopropyl alcohol. Using electrical tape, secure the cables to the channels along the top of the bars–many pro mechanics cover the bar with electrical tape all the way from the brake levers to where the cables exit the bars near the centre. With the new tape, begin at the open end of the bar and ensure that half the width overhangs the bar all the way around. There is no consensus on which way to tape bars but it's popular to tape away from the bike.

2 Start taping along the flat part of the bar, covering half the tape width with each turn as you work along the bar. Pull the tape tight. It depends on the type of tape how tight to wrap it but the important thing is to get it tight enough to prevent it unwrapping when it is being gripped. As the hands grip the bars they can exert a twisting force which can, over time, cause the tape to unravel.

3 Pull back the brake lever rubber hoods from the bar, exposing the body of the lever. This should have been done when removing the old tape as it's best not to have to let go of the tape after you have started wrapping it. It's important to maintain tension once the taping has started. If you do have to let it go, unwrap it a turn or two before continuing.

4 As the tape reaches the bar directly under the lever body go over the top, around the back of the bar, under the bar, then back over the top to make a figure of eight. How to tape around the levers is hotly contested, as you can just wrap the tape from below to above the lever, making sure to get the tape just overlapping the body and then use the 'cheat strip' to cover any gaps at the side.

5 Continue taping along the top of the bars. At the end of the taping continue at the same angle and cut the end into a 50mm (2in) taper. Pull it tight and seal the end with about two or three turns of electrical tape, cut as neatly as possible with the scissors. Finish the electrical tape just in front of the bottom of the bars. Rarely is the finishing tape supplied with bar tape worth using. It may look fancy but it can be almost impossible to pull tight around the tape. Fit the end plugs, making sure they are the correct way up if there is a logo on them. Pull back the rubber lever hoods.

▲ Replacing bar tape is a regular if not daily task at the Tour.

TOUR TIP

Before you start taping up the bars make sure you have scissors and insulating tape to cut and finish off the taping either right next to the bars or in your pockets.

CHAIN CHECKS

▲ Chains are also replaced at least once during the race.

1 Chains are joined using either a split or quick link or by pushing in a new rivet. If the chain has a quick link option this is the easiest way to fit a new one. A quick link can be fitted by hand but to remove one and split a chain it's worth using a quick link tool which resembles a pair of pliers with two pins that engage the links. To rivet a chain together, take it apart or make it shorter, you will need a riveting tool suitable for the size and possibly brand of chain. Removing a rivet can be done with a basic riveting tool but for certain chains like Campagnolo's 11-speed, the Campagnolo tool must be used to push in the rivet and then used on the other side to flatten it completely flush with the side plate.

2 On modern racing bikes with 10, 11 and now 12-speed cassettes, you must fit the correct chain which corresponds to the sprocket widths. All road chains are the same 12.5mm (½in) pitch but they vary in width depending on the number of sprockets. The safest way to replace a chain is to use the same brand which corresponds to the cassette and gears. There are quality alternatives to the drivetrain brands, however, which are also worth using but compatibility should be double-checked.

3 The easiest way to determine if a chain is worn is to use a chain checking tool which sits tightly between the links and shows whether the chain has gone beyond its wear limits. Once a chain is excessively worn it will not sit snugly on the teeth of the sprockets or the chainrings, accelerating wear in both components and requiring a much more expensive fix than if the chain had been replaced while within its limits.

4 Quick links should only be used with compatible chains and it's best to use a new one each time you renew a chain. Shimano, SRAM and KMC are three examples but there are many other brands with quick links. For a long time Shimano chains were rivet only but the recent addition of a quick link for 11-speed chains means you do not have to use the Shimano riveter. Shimano quick links are one use only. Campagnolo chains are joined with a rivet pin in the traditional way. A Campagnolo riveting tool should be used and the rivet cannot be re-used.

5 Split the chain with a quick link tool or sharp-nose pliers. The flat pins on the nose of the quick link pliers fit between the rollers either side of the split pin side plates. Holding the chain firmly with the tool directly beneath it, squeeze the pliers, compressing the split links until the rivet shifts along its slot and releases the split link.

6 Fitting a quick link is relatively easy. Once the correct chain length has been determined and links removed with a riveting tool, the side with the rivets is pushed into the exposed rollers on the ends of the chain to be joined. The quick link plate is snapped into place over the rivet ends and pressure on the pedals pulls it back along its slot to lock the plate in place.

7 Establishing the length of the chain can depend on your riding style and the combination of chainrings and sprockets. Even the height of the bottom bracket can affect how much chain is used from one extreme to another. If you like to use the big ring and big sprockets, an extra link can put less tension on the derailleur arm. This is preferable to a chain that is too short, favouring the small ring and smaller sprockets.

8 On a Campagnolo chain the links are joined with a chain specific riveting tool. The one-use rivet is pushed into the roller to join the chain. The tool is then removed and the pin, which can also be replaced if damaged or worn, is used to peen the end of the exposed rivet on the other side of the chain. This flattens the rivet head so that it sits flush against the plate and does not catch on the sprockets.

► Look after your chain, replace it regularly and it will prolong the life of the drivetrain many times over.

TOUR TIP Make sure the chain is fitted with the brand stamped on the outside facing plates, as some chains are direction sensitive.

CASSETTE REMOVAL AND CLEANING

▲ **Remember to clean and check the condition of the cassette hub.**

1 Tools for the removal of a cassette include various types of splined extractor tools which slide into the cassette lock ring and are turned by a big spanner or wrench. The Shimano splined tool is the most common and most pro mechanics will have a one-piece socket with a handle which makes cassette removal much faster and less likely to damage either the cassette or the mechanic's knuckles. The traditional chain whip is a universal tool and is the best way to lock the freewheel and allow the extractor to undo the cassette.

2 The lock ring holds the cassette in place. It tightens onto the smallest sprocket which, because the other sprockets are sitting securely on the splined cassette body, is enough to ensure all the sprockets are locked in place. Removing the lock ring takes both hands, one on the extractor tool turning anti-clockwise and the other on the chain whip opposing it in a clockwise direction. If separate extractor tool and wrench are being used, it's worth holding the extractor tool in place with the quick-release skewer. Remove the springs and put

the skewer through the hole on the extractor. Do up the nut until it just holds the tool in place. As soon as the lock ring comes loose, remove the skewer and unscrew the lock nut by hand.

3 With the lock ring removed, put the wheel on its side on a worktop and carefully lift off all the sprockets, which should slide easily up the cassette body. The sprockets are located on splines on the cassette body but there is one wider spline designed to correspond to a wider slot on the sprocket. There will also be spacers in between the single sprockets. Make sure you keep everything together; if you are storing the sprockets tie them together loosely with a zip-tie or piece of string.

4 Removal of the sprockets is the only way to deep clean them. Pro team bikes always have immaculate drivetrains with cassettes glittering with shiny sprockets. It is possible to keep a cassette free from hard deposits of oil and road grime without removing it from the wheel but to reach the middle of the bigger sprockets and really remove dirt between the spacers, the sprockets must be removed. Degrease them or clean them in a parts washer. Polish with a clean cloth and they will come up like new.

TOUR TIP Take a photo on your phone of the sprockets and spacers before you disassemble them as it can be a useful reference for putting them back together after cleaning.

REPLACING WORN COMPONENTS

▲ Make sure the wheel is upright and held securely when doing up the cassette lock ring.

5 Replacing a pile of sprockets and spacers looks daunting but is easy once you have a system in place. Lay the sprockets out on a worktop with spacers in between each single sprocket. With the wheel lying flat on the worktop, find the wide spline on the cassette body and turn the body until the spline is at 12 o'clock. Pick up the biggest sprocket and with its widest slot at 12 o'clock, locate the wide spline and slide it onto the cassette body. Continue down the sprockets, alternating single sprockets with spacers. Some sprockets may have flanged carriers which do not need a spacer. With all the sprockets and spacers in place the smallest sprocket should line up flush with the threaded edge of the body.

6 Carefully thread in the lock ring, insert the extractor tool and screw it in by hand until it is snug on top of the smallest sprocket. With an automotive torque wrench, typically set to 40Nm (29½ft-lb) and marked on the ring, do up the lock ring to the specified torque setting. It feels tight but it is important to follow the recommended loading as some cassettes have plastic spacers which are designed to compress to a certain width, ensuring the most precise synchronisation between the gears and sprockets.

BEARINGS AND TYPES

1 Here are a selection of tools for removing (pulling) and fitting (pressing) sealed bearings showing how specialist these tools are. Only the more committed home mechanics will have tools for replacing and servicing the bearings on a modern bike and most will be happy to pay a mechanic to service their bearings.

2 There are different size cartridge sealed bearings for the wheels, headset and bottom bracket and many variations within each component type, too. The bearing number should be marked on the bearing casing or seal and should be referenced whenever a replacement is ordered. Some component brands supply their own bearings but standard sealed bearings can also be ordered from a specialist bearing supplier.

3 Shimano still favours traditional cup and cone bearings on many of its wheels and many pro teams will upgrade the steel ball bearings for high performance ceramic replacements. Hubs with cup and cone bearings are better than sealed bearings at resisting axial loads and can also be adjusted and serviced more easily. A correctly adjusted and greased cup and cone bearing can run more smoothly than a sealed bearing.

3

▲ If the hub has loose ball bearings it may need cleaning and greasing.

4 A threadless headset is the universal bearing on a modern bike's steering system. The bearings in a threadless headset can last for years, with minimal wear due to their light loadings. Water ingress, however, will dry out and damage a sealed bearing, making it feel stiff and notchy. Replacement is the only option, as a damaged seal bearing is not worth trying to repair due to its low unit cost.

5 To adjust Shimano cup and cone wheel bearings first remove the quick-release skewers. Using a 5mm hex key, first unscrew the lock nut and dust cover to expose the cone. Note the way they sit on the hub axle and take a photo on your phone for peace of mind. Fit the exposed wheel axle on the other side into a vice.

6 Rock the rim gently and feel for any play. To take up any play it's possible to turn the serrated 'digital' style cones by hand while checking for play at the rim. Insert the hex key in the other side of the axle to stop it turning. If the hubs need greasing the cones and balls should be removed, cleaned, re-greased and replaced.

7 To adjust the hubs, undo the cone anti-clockwise and when the correct adjustment is found, click it back home fully. This system prevents the quick-release compressing the hubs when it is tightened. Checking for play is more important than feeling the bearings for smoothness as once the hub is correctly adjusted it will be as smooth as it can be.

8 Once the cones are correctly adjusted, make sure the axle is clean and the threads are free from dirt. A light coating of oil or grease will help the dust cover and lock nut go on smoothly and release more easily at the next service. Tighten the lock nut with the hex key to the specified torque.

TOUR TIP

Traditional hubs with loose ball bearings can be serviced with new bearings and fresh grease, and in some cases the bearing surfaces can be reground. In reality once a hub requires this level of repair it may be worth having the wheel rebuilt with new hubs or a complete replacement.

A high-speed mass pile-up is one of the most feared and damaging crashes.

TOUR de FRANCE™

CHAPTER 14

CRASH DAMAGE, CHECKS AND REPAIRS

In a peloton of 176 riders, all of them under pressure to work for their teams and win a stage, there are inevitably going to be crashes and it is a rare day at the Tour de France when there are no spills at all. Even the smallest crash can damage a carbon fibre bike with its exposed wheels and components. After a crash, the mechanics will closely inspect the bike for any part which may need replacing.

HOW CRASHES HAPPEN

Bike crashes are part of everyday life at the Tour de France, and with the proliferation of cameras, not just on motorbikes in front and behind the bunch but also in the air and on the bikes themselves, even the smallest spill usually makes it onto the daily round-ups. The most common type of crash is quite simply the result of having so many riders in close proximity. How fast they are going is immaterial – just look at how often there is a small crash after the bunch rolls away from the start, as it ambles along in the neutral zone before the 'depart reel'. One rider is looking down at something on his bike, the bunch slows down and before you know it there's a cyclist and bike lying upside down in the road while the whole Tour convoy slams on its brakes, cursing and spilling coffees. Meanwhile the TV cameras zoom in.

Lack of concentration is the most common reason for a mistake of this type and whenever there's a lull in the bunch, signalled by the peloton spreading right across the road, that is when small crashes occur. Damage to the bike in this type of spill can be minimal but that is not always the case for the rider, who can easily fall awkwardly and break a collarbone.

It sounds strange but when the peloton is going flat-out, at speeds over 65kph (40mph), there are very few crashes due to inattention. The riders are strung out in a line, riding as hard as they can and, with maximum concentration on the wheel in front, their reactions are usually good enough to avoid a crash.

At the Tour on a flat stage, the final hour is usually ridden flat-out. The first hour can be ballistic too. As soon as the flag is dropped, individual riders and teams fight to put together a breakaway. Riders attack and try to form a breakaway but if the peloton chases it down, another move goes clear

▲ A small crash may result in little more than a damaged or punctured wheel.

▶ When a dozen or more riders crash there is a high chance that bikes and wheels will be broken beyond repair.

▲ Incredibly, thanks to their lightning quick reactions, a high-speed crash in a sprint does not always result in other riders going down.

until the leaders in the bunch either run out of team-mates to chase, or decide the break is not a threat to their overall strategy.

At the end of the stage the sprinters' teams, as well as the teams of the overall leaders, mass at the front and ramp up the speed to bring back the breakaway and make it almost impossible for anyone else to get away.

It's when a fast moving bunch either slows down a little or encounters a roundabout, or the road narrows, that a big crash can bring down a lot of riders. This is the type of crash, apart from a solo rider flying off the side of a mountain pass, which the riders fear as they have no control over the outcome and can only hope for the best as they hurtle towards fallen riders and broken bikes.

There is also the danger of hitting something or somebody by the roadside like a spectator, post or parked car. There might be only a few high-speed crashes in the peloton during the Tour but they exact a high price in injuries and abandons, and written-off equipment.

When carbon fibre wheels and frames are involved in big impacts they can fail spectacularly, folding or shattering into an ugly mess of frayed carbon, and it's obvious to the mechanics rushing forward with spare wheels and bikes that wholesale replacements are required. But with a minor accident there may be little outward signs of damage and after a quick cursory check roadside, the rider will be pushed back into action. Later he may drift back to the team car for further checks and adjustments and might even swap to his spare bike just to be completely safe.

POST-CRASH CHECKS

GENERAL CHECKS

A small crash on the road will almost certainly leave some tell-tale marks which will not necessarily affect the performance of any of the components or the bike as a whole. The handlebar tape may be scuffed or torn and the same goes for the saddle. Tape will be replaced and so will the saddle.

There will often be scratches on the pedals and rear derailleur, both of which stick out and are the first components to hit the ground even when the bike just falls over. The brake lever tips and rubber hoods can also be scratched or damaged. All these components will be replaced even if the damage looks cosmetic and the machine has been ridden to the end of the stage. Without dismantling the component, there is always the risk of

there being more serious unseen damage, and it's also not in the team or bike sponsor's interests to present their bikes in anything less than immaculate order.

If the tyre is not punctured in the crash the first major components to check are the wheels. Even if there are no outward signs of damage – the tyre may have taken the brunt of the impact, for instance – the wheels should be spun in the frame to see if they are still running true and that the spokes are not damaged or broken. Inspect the rims for any cracks or bulges. Make sure the quick-release levers have not been dislodged in the crash and are still tight.

If the handlebars have taken some of the impact and there is damage to the bar tape, the bars should be examined closely for cracks or dents. Excess flex in the bars can indicate something more serious and the tape should be completely removed to confirm this. Many pro riders prefer to use

▲ Carbon frames can fail catastrophically in a crash.

aluminium handlebars over carbon fibre as they are less likely to fail catastrophically in a big crash and even if an aluminium bar is bent it can still be ridden until a spare bike is taken.

If the rear derailleur mechanism is scratched on the mounting bolt the impact may have damaged the derailleur itself or the hanger onto which it is bolted. The quickest way to check is by looking from behind at the alignment of the gear hanger, which should sit in-line and directly below each sprocket. If it is at an angle, the derailleur or the hanger may be bent and the only way to check is by taking the derailleur out and screwing in a gear hanger alignment tool. Riding with a bent rear derailleur will adversely affect gear changing and function and if the biggest sprocket is selected the gear hanger can go into the back wheel which, apart from jamming it, can cause considerable damage to the wheel, derailleur, hanger and even the frame.

Like the rear derailleur on the right hand side, the pedals on both sides cannot escape cosmetic damage if the bike slides down the road. Again that may not indicate that the pedals or the axles are seriously damaged or bent and usually they are not. But the mechanic will still double-check later to make sure the axle is not bent. Even if the scratches on a pedal look cosmetic, the mechanic will change the pedal as the risk of riding with a pedal which is not absolutely straight is not worth taking. Scratched and scuffed pedals look unsightly too.

CHECKING THE FRAME

After the wheels, the frame is the most important component to check immediately after a crash and then later, more forensically, after the stage. Carbon frames can take a lot of punishment in normal use and are also strong in a crash, especially if the bike has not been involved in a direct impact. If the frame is obviously so badly damaged or broken that it cannot

A. Scored rear derailleur

B. Scuffed carbon chainset

C. Mechanic checks for damage

D. Snapped carbon seat stay

149

CRASH DAMAGE, CHECKS AND REPAIRS

E. New bike please!

F. Mechanic checks bars

▶ When carbon fails, it can be spectacular and catastrophic, as this broken machine shows after a big impact.

be ridden, the rider will take a spare bike from the mechanic and the written-off bike will go back onto the roof rack. After the stage the frame will be stripped of all its components, some or all of which can be re-assembled on a new frame.

The fork can be damaged if the bike has hit anything head-on. Check the orientation of the fork legs to each other and that they can still turn smoothly in the head tube. Steel forks can be bent backwards after a head-on impact but a carbon fork could spring back yet still sustain a potentially dangerous failure later. Even pro mechanics admit that it can be very difficult to identify hairline cracks in carbon parts and they will always play safe in the event of an impact, swapping out the fork or frame. One simple way to test for possible damage is to lightly tap around the suspected area with a heavy coin, listening for any variation in the tone of the tapping sound which could indicate an internal crack.

It is not possible to check the steerer tube inside the head tube until after the race but if there has been a heavy front-end crash it is imperative to take the fork out and examine it very closely for any cracks. Where the fork crown meets the steerer is the highest stress point. Modern carbon frames have very stiff head tubes which put more load on the fork in the event of a crash.

If the fork has taken the impact, the area of the frame directly behind the head tube can also sustain damage and should be checked for any cracks or bulges. If the frame is painted it is easier to spot cracked or crazed paint or lacquer. It is possible that a light impact may only have cracked the exterior lacquer and that the carbon beneath it is undamaged. The only way to ascertain the true extent of any damage is to take the frame to a professional carbon fibre repairer. With a thermographic X-ray camera, heat is applied to the area which will highlight a crack under the camera as the heat dissipates. Ultrasound and conventional X-ray can also be used to detect internal damage. Specialists may also use microscopic imaging to review hairline cracks.

In a crash the front wheel often turns to full lock and the handlebars can impact heavily with the top tube. Check this point on both sides of the top tube for any signs of crash damage. Normally the cushioning in the bar tape protects the top tube from a potential frame repair or write-off.

In a pile-up type crash the bike may not sustain a big impact but sustain damage from other bikes and riders falling on the bike. Check the rest of the frame for any signs of damage, especially the fragile seat stays and along the whole of the exposed top tube.

The single most checked, fitted and prepared part of a Tour bike are its tyres. Every day, mechanics will perform multiple tyre-related tasks.

CHAPTER 15:

TYRES AT THE TOUR

Cycle racing at the highest level shares the same obsession with tyres as motorsports like Formula One and Moto GP. Tyre choice, inflation pressures and daily checks consume much of the Tour de France mechanic's time and there is lots for the enthusiast to learn from their almost fanatical attention to detail. Technological advances in recent years seem to have benefitted enthusiasts more than pros but change is coming to this most traditional part of a pro bike team.

TYRES AT THE TOUR

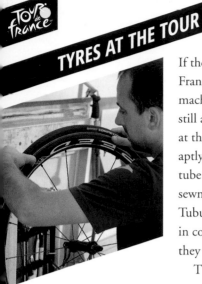

▲ **Tubular tyre fitting is a skilled job that takes practice to master.**

If there is one thing which sets a Tour de France bike apart from an enthusiast's machine it is the tyres. Tubular tyres are still almost universally favoured by teams at the Tour. Also known as sew-ups, this aptly describes the construction of an inner tube encased in an outer cover which is sewn together and sealed with a base tape. Tubular tyres are more than a century old in concept and there are good reasons why they are rarely used outside of pro racing.

They are laborious to repair when punctured, because the base tape must be carefully peeled back before the thread can be cut and then unpicked to access the inner tube. The inner tube cannot be replaced and although it can be patched in the conventional manner, two or three inches of the casing must then be sewn back together and the base tape stuck back on. In practice, a punctured tubular tyre is usually thrown away. Pro team mechanics will always discard a punctured tub, they just do not have time to repair them and the risk of a failed repair is not worth the trouble.

Quality handmade tubulars are also expensive even when compared to the combined price of a lightweight inner tube and clincher or wired-on tyre. There really is little point to a budget tubular tyre because the extra weight and lesser quality materials cancel out two of the most important features of a top road tubular.

There are enthusiasts who would be happy to pay extra for a tyre, even one which you have to replace after a single puncture. The deal breaker, however, is that tubular tyres are not fitted dry to the rim as is the case with an 'open' tyre on a clincher

or radial rim. A tubular tyre must be glued to a rim designed purely for tubular tyres. Not just with one layer of specialist glue, either, the rim must also be prepared with a thin bed of the same glue, then left to cure overnight.

Mounting the tyre is also a skilled job, as the tyre must be stretched beforehand and care must be taken not to smear glue all over the sides of the tyre before it is expertly centred on the rim. Twenty-five years ago tubular tyres were the only choice for amateur racers and professionals. Since then, the ease of fitment and repair, quality and technological advances in clincher tyres has made the tubular virtually redundant among enthusiast riders.

TUBULAR TYRES RULE

So why do cyclists in the Tour de France continue to favour tubular tyres over clinchers? There is no single knockout reason, as you might expect when the argument for clincher and more recently radial tyres is so compelling. Not surprisingly the performance margins are now so small as to be negligible. Research on rolling resistance for both types of tyre has put high performance clinchers ahead of tubulars. But professional cyclists still say they prefer the feel and handling properties of a tubular and what they say counts, because having absolute confidence in your choice of tyre is everything when your livelihood depends on it.

If there is one unique advantage of a tubular over a clincher it is the ability of a tubular to withstand an impact puncture. A pinch puncture is when the tyre is pushed back by a hard edge until it contacts

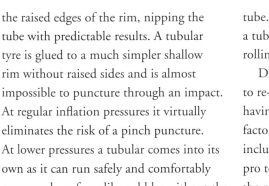

the raised edges of the rim, nipping the tube with predictable results. A tubular tyre is glued to a much simpler shallow rim without raised sides and is almost impossible to puncture through an impact. At regular inflation pressures it virtually eliminates the risk of a pinch puncture. At lower pressures a tubular comes into its own as it can run safely and comfortably over rough surfaces like cobbles without the much higher risk of pinch punctures run by clinchers.

Another advantage of the simple box section rim with a shallow concave bed on which the tubular tyre sits, is that when a tubular tyre does go down, it rests against the carbon or alloy rim, ensuring the hard surface of the rim does not make contact with the road. This allows the cyclist to stay upright and continue riding on a flat tyre. Both are very important to a Tour rider who needs to maintain control of his bike and lose as little time as possible as he drops behind and continues riding until his team car can come up the line and perform a wheel change. When a clincher tyre deflates the tyre loses its shape and the hard rim edges can contact the road making the bike dangerously hard to control.

NEW TYRE TECH

Tubular tyres, like the glue that sticks them to a rim, are hanging on tenaciously in the pro peloton of the Tour but recent advances in tyre and braking tech could begin to weaken their grip. Two things in particular are making inroads on pro teams. Tubeless tyres look like a clincher tyre but are designed to create an airtight seal on the rim and, as a result, do not need an inner

tube. They offer many of the advantages of a tubular as well as the holy grail of lower rolling resistance.

Disc brakes are freeing up designers to re-imagine the traditional rim without having to include a braking surface or factor in the effects of heat build-up. If you include the addition of electronic gears on pro team bikes, the current era is one of the most exciting times in the evolution of the bicycle.

A bicycle tubeless tyre requires a rim very similar to a clincher version with raised sides to secure the bead of the tyre. A tubeless compatible rim, however, is designed for an airtight seal between the rim sides and the bead of the tyre. The bed of the rim is also airtight, with covered spoke holes and a joint-free finish. This allows the radial tyre to be mounted and inflated without an inner tube. There are several advantages to tubeless tyres: they are light, can be as supple as a tubular and are almost as impervious to pinch flats due to the absence of an inner tube.

▼ Checking by eye that the tyre is sitting correctly on the rim.

As a result, radials can be run safely and comfortably at lower tyre pressures, again, just like a quality tubular tyre. Rolling resistance is, if anything, better than a tubular which suffers friction losses through its inner tube and bonded connection to the rim. Like a clincher tyre, a radial can also be designed to create a more aerodynamic shape when mounted on a wider modern rim.

RESISTANCE TO TUBELESS

Professional cycling has been slow to adopt radial tyres which are now widely available from rim and tyre manufacturers. There have been some compatibility issues but the extra rim weight and unpredictable handling when they do go down, are issues that have not been resolved. For enthusiast riders, tubeless are an excellent choice, especially if the tyre is filled with sealant which virtually eliminates the risk of being stranded by a puncture. Radials can be hard to mount on the rim, however, and they also need a strong initial blast of inflation to establish an airtight seal between the bead and rim.

Heat build-up from heavy and prolonged braking with rim brakes is another reason why Tour riders and mechanics prefer to stick with what they know and trust – tubulars – over radials and clincher tyres. Carbon rims are less efficient at dissipating heat than alloy versions and long mountain descents are where heat build-up puts tyres and latex inner tubes under high stress. Tyres secured with beads, clinchers and tubeless, can start to bulge or even blow off the rim. Tubulars and rims prepared by professional Tour mechanics continue to offer consistent performance and security, but the spread of disc brakes in the peloton has given bike designers a chance to rethink the traditional role of the rim as well as its relationship with the tyre. Removing the need for a rim to provide a braking surface means they can be made lighter and in a shape designed to optimise the aerodynamics between the tyre and rim. Of course, it also means that rims for tubular tyres can take advantage of a lighter, more aero, rim which will be attractive to riders looking for wheels with the lowest centrifugal mass offering maximum accelerative effect, especially on mountain climbs.

Another advantage of disc brakes is that, without the need to package a traditional caliper around the tyre at the top of fork and around the seat stays, these areas are now freed up, allowing the fitment of much wider or fatter tyres. Regular tyre sizes have already gone up to 23mm to 25mm (1in) or more, and for rough or cobbled stages there are now clearances to allow tyres of around 30mm (1¼in). Contrary to received wisdom, a bigger tyre at a lower inflation pressure need not affect rolling resistance and can actually roll faster than a narrow tyre at higher pressures.

Tubular tyres, despite their drawbacks, still offer the best combination of lightness, feel and safety for professional riders in the Tour de France. There are exciting alternatives which perform equally as well or better than a tubular, but it could be a while before pro teams feel confident enough in how safely they can be ridden when flat before they make the big change.

Time trialling is the one discipline at the Tour in which the lower rolling resistance of a clincher or radial tyre is hard to argue against, as the issues affecting these tyres on a road stage do not apply. There is no need to ride far on the rim in the rare event of a puncture, as there is a following car just metres behind in a time trial. Heavy braking downhill and heat build-up is rare in a time trial, and the lightest rim and tyre combination is unnecessary as hard accelerations are not required in a TT. Tour mechanics on certain teams will have a stock of time trial wheels fitted with high performance clincher or tubeless tyres.

TOUR MECHANICS AND TYRES

Of all the daily jobs of the Tour mechanic, working with tyres is the most time consuming. From pumping them up at the beginning of the day, to changing punctured wheels during the stage and then replacing tyres and preparing rims later the same evening, every day is a tyre day at the Tour. Cycling may not have the same win or lose relationship with tyres that afflicts motorsport of every shade, but as with any two-wheeled activity, when the only connection between the rider and the road is a relatively tiny contact patch of rubber, every effort is made to maximise performance and grip.

A slight difference in tyre compound is unlikely to affect the outcome of a race as it can in motorsport. But in cycling the wrong tyre choice or pressure could result in a puncture or crash with serious consequences for the rider. Tyre choice in cycling is almost never attributed to a stage

win, but a problem with tyres can most certainly adversely affect a rider's prospects in the Tour de France.

Team mechanics have an endless variety of jobs to get through every day and they are used to working with expert speed. But there are times when the onlooker will see them visibly slow down and take on the measured pace of a true craftsman. More often than not it's when they are inspecting tyres, preparing and fitting them to rims and checking tyre pressures to the nearest psi. There are many components on the modern Tour bike which require little or no maintenance or, as is the case with electronic gears, will even self-adjust. Faulty equipment is simply replaced and some of the traditional skills of the pro bike mechanic are rarely called upon. Maybe that is why mechanics at the Tour still take a lot of pride in the one component that has barely changed in over a century and which demands age-old skills of preparation and care.

▲ Spare wheels with tyres suited to the stage are put onto the roof racks of team cars.

GLUE AND TIME

Every team at the Tour comes to the race with a truck filled with wheels shod with new tyres as well as up to 100 new tyres to be used over the three-week race. Tyres will be replaced after punctures or when they are worn or show signs of damage. In wet weather, time trials and special stages over cobbles or dirt roads, the team will also have suitable wheels and tyres prepared.

Every team will have mechanics working shifts on tyres throughout the Tour, removing tyres and methodically preparing rims before fitting new ones. A rim fitted with a tubular tyre will have at least three thin layers of special rim cement applied and, once the old tyre has been pulled off, some of the old glue is

▼ Glue is applied to the tubular tyre as well as the rim bed.

scraped off to prepare the rim bed for a fresh application of glue.

With the wheel in a jig for ease of access, the mechanic uses a blade or a file to pare down the old glue before carefully applying tubular specific glue with a small brush. On new rims the mechanic may use a wire brush to key the surface prior to its first layer of glue. At the same time as the rim, a thin layer of glue is also applied to the inside of a pre-stretched tubular tyre, which has also had any glaze taken off it with a light file.

Rim cement does not go completely hard and remains sticky for a long time. At least three layers are applied to a new rim and, each time a layer is applied, the wheel is put to one side to allow the glue to cure for 24 hours. When the rim is ready, a final layer of glue is applied and left for a few minutes to dry to a sticky finish. The partially inflated tyre is then mounted on the rim and carefully centred by eye. More air is added, about 20psi, while the mechanic continues to centre the tyre on the still tacky rim bed. He will check for a lateral movement in the tread as well as any bumps, usually around the valve. Excess glue is carefully wiped off with a rag soaked in acetone. The tyre is mounted on the rim but ideally it should be left to cure for another two days before being ridden.

TOUR TIP

Some mechanics use a thumb to apply the final layer of glue, ensuring it's as thin as can be with no excess.

TUBULAR TYRE FITTING

1 Make sure the tubular tyre has a long enough valve for the intended rim. Deep carbon rims require very long valve stems. Pro mechanics can graft extensions onto standard length valves as there are multiple rim depth options in a Tour team truck. Stretch a new tubular tyre on a spare wheel without recent glue on the rim.

2 Put the wheel in a trueing jig if possible. If the wheel is new, the rim bed may have a shiny finish which will need to be keyed before the first layer of glue is applied. Use a wire brush to roughen up the surface, carefully running the brush up and down the centre of the curved bed.

3 If the wheel is not new and has old layers of tubular glue on the rim, some or all of the old glue needs to be removed. Scrape off excess glue with a short blade, either until there is a level but thin layer of old glue left, or until the old glue is completely removed.

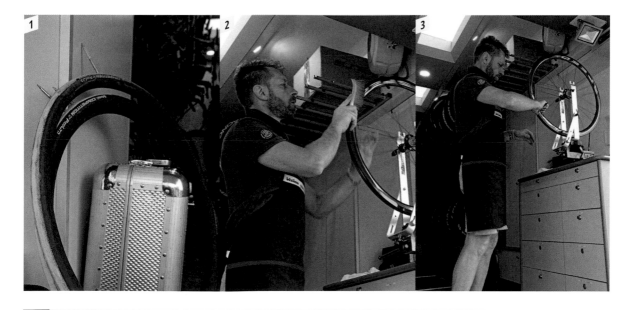

TOUR TIP

If possible, store quality new tubulars unboxed in a dark, dry place where the rubber will not deteriorate. Mount them dry on rims to stretch them before fitting.

4 When the rim is prepared the first layer of new glue can be applied. Using a small brush, spread a thin layer evenly around the rim, taking care to avoid the spoke holes but making sure there is glue around the valve hole. Some mechanics use a cycling or cleaned sauce bottle filled with glue, squeezing a small blob out between each spoke hole.

5 Remove any glazing on the inside base tape of the tubular tyre using a fine file and apply a thin layer of glue to the base tape. Allow the glue to cure on the rim and the tyre for 24 hours. Repeat the glueing process one or two more times on a new rim. Glue the base tape one more time.

6 Apply a final layer of glue to the rim and leave for a few minutes or until the glue feels tacky. Make sure you have a clean dry surface, or something like a front wheel stand for use with a turbo trainer on which the rim can stand while the tyre goes on.

7 Put a small amount of air into the tyre, just enough to give it shape. Insert the valve into the hole and, with the wheel on the ground directly in front of you, put the top half of the tyre onto the rim making sure the valve is straight.

8 Hold the wheel against your waist and work the tyre onto the other half of the rim. Get it as central on the rim as possible, using the edge of the base tape as a guide. Use your hands to feel around the tyre and make sure the tyre is sitting snugly in the rim bed.

9 Put 20psi in the tyre and turn the wheel slowly and check that the tread is running straight by looking along it. Check also that there are no bumps in the tyre, especially around the valve. While the glue is still curing the tyre can be moved around until it is running straight on the rim.

10 Pump the wheel up to riding pressure and check the rim for excess glue which can be carefully scraped off or removed with acetone on a rag. Braking will also remove excess glue from the rim. Leave the wheel for 24 hours before riding.

TOUR TIP

You can't repair a tubular tyre out on the road, so the only solutions are to either fit a spare tubular and ride home very carefully or re-inflate the punctured tyre with tubular tyre sealant in an aerosol can.

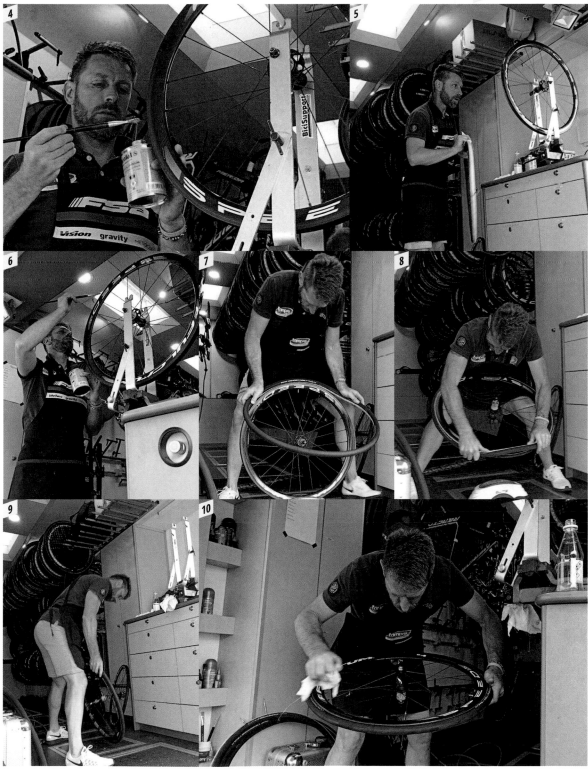

One-off paint and special details make the Tour de France bikes stand out from the rest.

CHAPTER 16

PERSONALISING YOUR BIKE

A Tour de France bike has a number of customised components, many of which are so subtle only an expert can spot them. There are some things that a pro mechanic will do to make their bikes stand out, and these can be fun to incorporate on your own bike. Looks may not be everything but when it comes to bikes, however, if it looks right it usually goes right!

PERSONALISING YOUR BIKE

▲ **Many riders have their own personalised logo or graphic applied to the frame.**

How do you make your bike stand out from the rest? This is increasingly something to which cyclists are turning their attention and the bike industry has been quick to respond to the demand for parts, accessories and services that personalise and customise the modern machine. Mass-produced carbon fibre frames and the popularity of a small number of groupset brands has resulted in a loss of the hand-crafted individuality of hand built steel frames, the only option before the 1990s. In those pre-carbon days there were frame builders in every region of every cycling-mad country and most hand built frames were sized, specced and painted to individual customer order.

After being measured up for a tailor-made frame, the customer of a frame builder would then specify which tubing to be used, the method of joining them (with lugs or without), any 'fancy' detailing to the lugs and forks and also the type and design of the dropouts. Even the type of cable guides could be specced, as well as how the cables were routed along the top and down tubes. Finally, there was an almost endless choice of colours to choose from and even the style and colour of the frame builder's graphics. Older steel frames could also be given a new lease of life with a re-spray and new graphics, all in fresh colours of course.

EXCLUSIVE COLOURS

Carbon frames can be custom painted and re-sprayed and if there is one way to make your factory-built frame stand out from the crowd, a re-spray is the most strikingly visual. They can also be repaired and as carbon has become the universal material of choice for serious riders, there has been a corresponding growth in specialist bike frame repairers and painters. Carbon frames are more sensitive to stripping and paint types so you should only use an expert in carbon fibre repairs and finishing for any of these jobs. It is not prohibitively expensive to get a frame re-sprayed but don't forget to also budget for the components to be removed and put back by a pro mechanic.

Some major bike brands also offer custom paint options and if you want to create your own limited edition machine, while also retaining its authenticity, it's worth tracking one down. If they offer bespoke build options, you can have the bicycle equivalent of a luxury motorcar.

CUSTOM CARBON

Not all carbon fibre frames are mass-produced in factories from a limited selection of moulds. A small number of artisan frame builders working with carbon fibre can create a frame tailored to your exact dimensions in a very similar way to a traditional steel frame builder. The most favoured method for making custom carbon frames is to use tube-to-tube construction, which allows the builder to cut tubes to any length according to the individual customer. Not only that, as there are no moulds or lugs, the builder is free to create a unique geometry to suit the riding style of the rider. A very light frame can be made by hand because the builder has the luxury to select lighter tubes and spend more time and expertise paring down extraneous material than would ever be possible on a factory-

produced frame. Add to that a totally custom paintjob and a hand-built carbon frame is one of the most exclusive, and expensive, ways to set yourself apart from the crowd.

Even professional riders do not get this level of equipment, as their big brand bike partners cannot be seen to be supplying a frame that is not available in the shops. The frames ridden in the Tour de France are some of the lightest and best performing frames in cycling, but they are not always a perfect fit for every rider, which explains why Tour mechanics sometimes go to extreme lengths to fit and modify components to achieve the rider's perfect bike fit.

Custom paint finishes do appear on Tour de France bikes and are de rigueur for the wearers of the yellow, green and polka dot jerseys. Suitably painted in the colours of the jerseys, these machines attract much attention and are great publicity for the bike makers.

MIX AND MATCH

A regular Tour bike may not have custom paint but it will always have the name of the rider on the top tube and that is something which the regular cyclist can have too. In the Tour, it is absolutely essential that each bike is identified by the team mechanics who will have individual set-ups and preferences for all eight riders on the team. In the high pressure environment of the Tour the mechanic cannot afford to waste valuable

A. Etched headset top cap

B. Carbon saddle base

C. Bespoke green spot paint

time identifying a bike. For the casual rider or amateur racer, there are sticker manufacturers who will print your name, national flag or graphic and supply you with a set of stickers to personalise your frame.

Clear protective tape can also be used to protect the frame and parts from getting scratched. Use it on bars and seatposts under lights and computer clamps. For the frame there are clear protective sticker packs which can be used to stop cables from rubbing on the paint and are especially effective around the sides of the head tube.

Colour co-ordinating a bike is another fun way to personalise an off-the-peg machine and need not cost very much. Swapping the original bottle cage bolts for anodised replacements in a colour

▲ A colour-matched seat clamp.

▶ Cables with a heat shrink tube.

▶▶ Custom paint and graphics option.

matching the frame graphics is easy and if the correct bolts can be sourced, can be applied to other components like the chainring, stem and handlebars. Handlebar tape, of course, is another very affordable way to add colour but be aware that it can look like a cheap fix and that coloured bar tape can be hard to keep clean. Other components like stems, bars, seatposts and especially saddles are available in different colours and can transform the look of a bike if matched stylishly with the frame colour.

CABLE TIDYING

If your bike has electronic gears the thin cables from the bars to the frame can look exposed and untidy. One very neat solution is to route them alongside the brake cables through lengths of cable heat-shrinked from the bars to the entry ports on the frame. This is a fiddly job and must be done when the wires and cables are being routed through the frame. Heat-shrink tubing is available from electronic suppliers and is designed to slip over multiple wires. When heat is applied, the tube shrinks around the wires, effectively sealing them together. A hot air gun should be used to shrink the tube. Some teams also use a spiral plastic protective outer which is easier to fit over the cables and also does a good job of tidying them up.

TOUR TIP

Regular riders do not usually need to 'slam' their stems so that they sit almost directly on top of the head tube. But spacers under the stem do not look very 'pro' so a custom spacer is a clever way to hide a stack of spacers under the stem.

CLINCHER TYRE FITTING

▲ Tyre fitting and correcting tyre pressures is the one essential skill that every cyclist should master.

1 Check that the rim tape is in good condition and centrally mounted around the rim bed. Make sure the tape is covering all the spoke holes, as any exposed spoke ends can cause multiple punctures. Check the condition of the tape at the hole around the valve area. If the rim tape is damaged or perished replace it.

2 Examine the tyre and look for any direction arrows or markings which indicate which way the tyre should go on the rim. A tyre with a tread pattern will often be designed to work best in the direction of travel. If the tyre is used, check it for wear and pick out any foreign objects embedded in the carcass.

3 Line up the tyre make and model graphics next to the valve hole on the rim. This not only looks good, it makes it easier to locate a puncture relative to the valve and graphics. This is best done with the wheel on the floor, resting upright against the legs with the valve hole at the top.

4 Starting opposite the valve, ease the bead onto the rim using your thumbs and work the tyre onto the wheel. It should go on easily as it is only one side at first and without an inner tube. Push the last part of the tyre over the rim.

5 With the wheel and tyre half on, put a little pile of talc on the inside of the tyre. Any cheap talc will do, just make sure there is something under the wheel to catch any that spills out.

6 Using your fingers, work the talc around the entire circumference of the tyre. The talc prevents the inner from sticking to the tyre and can prevent damage and punctures.

TOUR TIP

You don't need to use the valve lock unless the valve is short and can only just be gripped by the pump chuck. It can also corrode in winter. However, in winter conditions a dust cap can protect the delicate valve barrel from corroding.

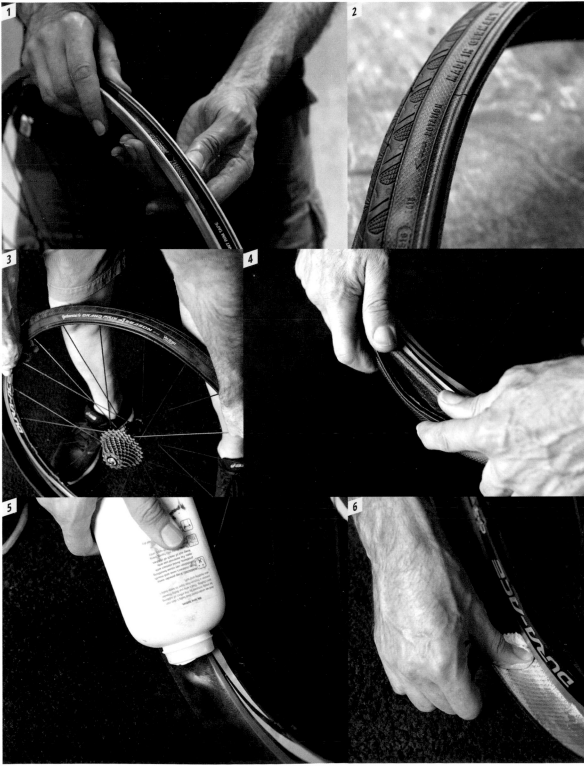

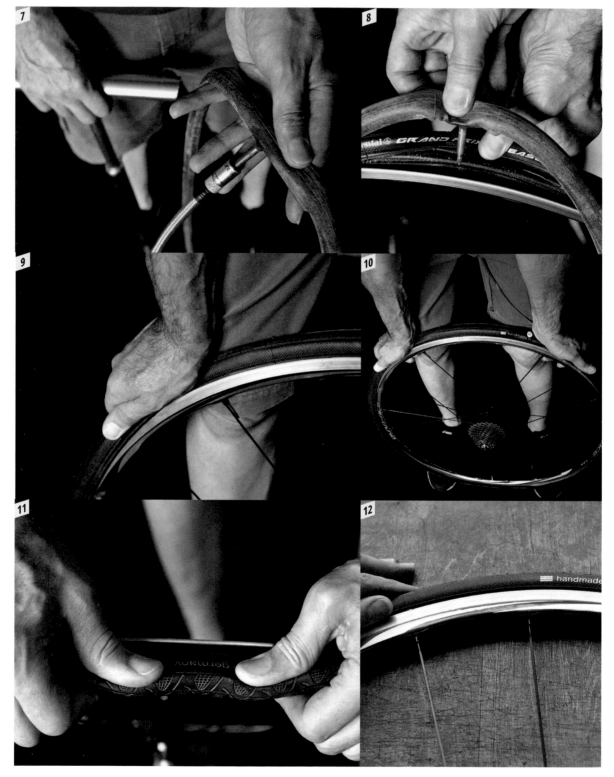

7 Make sure you have an inner tube with a long enough valve stem for your rims. Open out the inner tube. Undo the dust cap and lock nut from the valve. With a pump, put in just enough air to give it shape. Some people do this by mouth but it's not advisable if the tube has already been used. There are various ways to prevent annoying valve rattle but the simplest is to cut a centimetre square of insulating tape, carefully pierce it in the centre and pull it down over the top of the valve. Secure the tape on the rim and around the base of the valve.

8 Insert the inner tube valve under the tyre and into the valve hole. Push the tube into the tyre all the way around. Make sure the inner tube is pushed right into the tyre and is not twisted or bulging out in any places. Check that the valve is straight.

9 Fitting the tyre. Start opposite the valve and, with your thumbs, push the bead over the rim, working back towards the valve. Do not use levers if you can help it, the tyre should go on without needing them and there is a risk of a pinch puncture between the lever and inner tube.

10 If the tyre has seated on the rim it should be possible to use your thumbs to flip the final part of the bead at the valve. Push the tyre into the rim. Talcing the tyre helps and make sure there is not too much air in the inner tube. Let some out if there is. If you do have to use a tyre lever, a thin quality lever is worth spending extra on.

11 Before putting air into the tyre, methodically go around the tyre checking that it has seated on the rim and there is no inner tube showing under the bead. Using coloured rim tape can help spot a snagged tube. Go around the tyre, pinching and pulling upwards from the tread. This pulls the inner tube into the tyre, away from the bead.

12 Pump up the tyre with a floor or track pump. Pump to about half the recommended pressure and inspect the tyre, checking for any bulges and looking for a consistent line along the tyre which indicates whether it has seated correctly on the rim. If there is a bulge in the tyre caused by a pinched inner tube, let the tyre down completely and pinch the inner tube into the tyre again.

▲ A patch to stop valve rattling on rim.

TOUR TIP

Valve rattle is very irritating, but it can be solved easily by applying a patch or small square of insulating tape over the valve and securing it tightly around the base. Make sure the area around the rim is clean and dry and that the valve is snug against the patch.

1980s Colnago Mexico with Campagnolo groupset is one of the finest examples of a late model traditional road race bike.

CHAPTER 17:

CLASSIC RACE BIKES

Bicycles that have been raced in previous Tours are prized for their rarity and evocation of 'the heroic' eras of cycling, from the early 1950s to late 1980s. They are rare and highly collectable but the next best thing is a machine from the past with a similar specification to a Tour bike. The astonishing growth in recent years of Eroica rides and festivals, where classic racing bikes are ridden and celebrated, has generated even more interest in classic racing bikes and their maintenance.

1950s

As Europe continued to recover from the Second World War, the 1950s became a time of optimism and innovation in the bicycle industry, especially in its heartlands in Italy and France. In Italy, in 1950, the world leading component manufacturer, Campagnolo, influenced by the French Simplex gear derailleur, introduced the first reliable and robust cable-operated rear derailleur. The Gran Sport replaced the Campagnolo Cambio Paris-Roubaix system which used a rod attached to the rear seat stay, moving the wheel back and forth in the dropouts while a fork shifted the chain across four sprockets.

Derailleur rear gears with a spring-loaded parallelogram design represented a big step in the evolution of racing bike gears which have, in cable-operated form,

▲ **Campagnolo Paris-Roubaix derailleur.**

▼ **1950s Bianchi.**

barely changed to the present day. This Italian Bianchi from the early 1950s is not fundamentally so different to bikes ridden in the Tour de France nearly 50 years later. Even today there remain many similarities in how bikes function. From chain drive to cable-operated brakes and spoked wheels with tubular tyres, the only changes in half a century are to the quality of materials. How they function is broadly the same – a good testament to the fact that many components on the modern bike are so highly evolved that they are hard to improve upon.

The Bianchi's drivetrain, consisting of cable-operated front and rear derailleurs, a chainset with two chainrings and a cassette or block with sprockets in various tooth sizes, will be familiar to today's bike riders. There are only five sprockets on the Bianchi, giving the rider a choice of eight usable gears without running the chain

at an acute angle. Modern machines have 11 or 12 sprockets with 20 potential gear choices and if the derailleurs are cable operated, the levers will not be located on the down tube but incorporated into the brake levers. On the Bianchi, the rider must take his hands off the bars and reach down to move, with thumb and forefinger, dainty alloy paddles operating the rear derailleur on the right hand side and the front changer on the left.

There was no indexing on early derailleurs. The levers moved through a smooth arc pulling the derailleur up and down the block. Riders became adept at fine-tuning their gear changes with a micro fore-aft movement each time they swapped sprockets. The front derailleur required the same skills and the design of both derailleurs demanded considerably more finesse and mechanical sympathy than contemporary gear trains.

Braking was cable operated with alloy calipers located on the fork crown and the rear seat stay bridge. Many Tour de France bikes of the current era have the same braking system! The only differences are in the quality of materials and the addition of pivots in the caliper, which have enhanced brake feel and power.

There are other components on bikes from the 1950s which have not changed, proof if it was needed that despite attempts over the years, certain parts of the bike are beyond improvement. Take the design of the saddle and seatpost, for instance. On the old bike the top is made from comfortable and breathable leather mounted on twin rails secured to the top of the seatpost with a one- or two-bolt clamp.

Apart from the materials, the modern saddle and seatpost are basically of the same design. Even the seatpost, which can be adjusted simply and securely by sliding it up and down the seat tube, remains the most popular way to offer variations in saddle height required by racing cyclists.

The materials used in its construction are how the 1950s bike differs from modern machines. Whereas today carbon fibre is used for many parts including the frame, in the 1950s the whole peloton in the Tour rode on frames brazed together from steel tubes by expert craftsmen who displayed their skills with hand-filed lugs and finishes. Other parts, from the wheel rims to the handlebars and stem, were made from aluminium and considered exotic at the time. Wheels were lighter and stronger than before, but still relatively fragile and, with 36 spokes, not remotely aerodynamic. Today's Tour mechanic, however, would be instantly familiar with the rims and tubular tyres, which were prepared and stuck on with sticky rim cement in the same laborious process, with virtually no changes in technique in more than 70 years.

▲ Bar mounted alloy bottle on a 1950s Bianchi.

TOUR WINNERS DURING THE 1950S

1950, Ferdinand Kubler (Swi)
1951, Hugo Koblet (Swi)
1952, Fausto Coppi (Ita)
1953, Louison Bobet (Fra)
1954, Bobet
1955, Bobet
1956, Roger Walkowiak (Fra)
1957, Jacques Anquetil (Fra)
1958, Charly Gaul (Lux)
1959, Federico Bahamontes (Spa)

▲ A traditional seat lug with clamp and bolt.

Racing bicycles in the Tour de France continued to evolve slowly throughout the decade, with advances in materials and manufacturing more influential in effecting change than any radical advances in technology. Fundamentally, the bike was still handmade from steel with cable-operated derailleur gears and brakes. Thanks to improving road surfaces and higher quality steel tubesets, frame builders began to construct frames with shorter wheelbases which handled better than older frames designed primarily for comfort on rough surfaces. Seat tube angles became less laid back, pulling the back wheel tighter to the rear triangle and placing the rider more 'on top' of the pedals. Fork rake was reduced from the springy and slow steering forks of before. As speeds went up in the professional bunch, the bikes evolved to allow riders to react quicker to a more lively peloton and faster mountain descents.

One of the most striking visual differences of bikes of this era was the widespread adoption of centre-pull brakes, which had been around for many years but became the brake of choice for many pro teams during the 1960s. Centre-pull brakes were symmetrical cantilever brakes which were easier to align with the rims and provided more predictable and powerful braking than side-pull calipers. French and Italian manufacturers, Mafac and Universal, dominated and the introduction of soft rubber hoods also greatly improved comfort when the rider gripped the brake lever hand-holds. Centre-

pull brakes ruled the peloton until the end of the decade when Italian component maker Campagnolo introduced its Record brakeset, a high quality lightweight side-pull caliper design which put the side-pull brake back on top for decades to come.

Campagnolo were the first manufacturer to develop the concept of a groupset, a number of matching drivetrain and individual components which would go a long way to building up a complete bike from a bare frame. Through the 1950s, after the introduction of the Gran Sport derailleur, they added pedals, seatpost, the headset bearing assembly and chainset. In 1962, the Record derailleur improved shift quality and by 1963, of the 130 riders in the Tour de France, 110 had Campagnolo Record derailleurs fitted. Still, there were only five sprockets to choose from on the rear wheel.

Aluminium alloy parts largely replaced steel during the 1960s. In particular, the traditional steel chainset and cranks secured with a protruding cotter-pin was superseded by much better looking cotterless versions in alloy, fixed to square taper axles and with alloy chainrings. Stronglight chainsets were a popular fitment at the time, and with Mafac and Simplex also French made, the Italians did not have it all their own way. French Tour winners, led by Jacques Anquetil and Roger Pingeon in the 1960s, used Simplex gears and the French manufacturer held out against Italy with three more wins thanks to Bernard Thevenet in 1975 and 1977, and Laurent Fignon, who won his first Tour on Simplex gears in 1983.

Alloy handlebars and stems also

reduced weight and increased the choices of bar shape and stem lengths. Alloy bars and stems were not new, they had been around since the 1930s, but when Italian manufacturer Cinelli introduced their lightweight and elegant bars in the early 1960s they quickly found favour with pro riders. Matched with the iconic Cinelli 1A stem, the front end controls were much tidied up and would not change significantly for another 20 years. The Cinelli 1A stem differed from earlier alloy stems which had heavily styled forgings. It was smooth with a satin finish and the top of the expander bolt was recessed and was secured with a hex key.

Wheel technology edged forward during the 1960s with French manufacturer Mavic introducing the double-eyeleted rim, which further improved the alloy tubular rim, making it lighter and stronger when built up. A rim with double eyelets spreads the load of the spoke when it is tensioned in the rim. As a result, the rim can be more uniform in design and thus lighter. This design remains popular in aluminium rims today and Mavic wheels are widely used at the Tour de France. Mavic's famous yellow neutral service cars are one of the Tour's most loyal partners and can be seen on every stage rescuing stranded riders with spare Mavic wheels and yellow spare bikes.

TOUR WINNERS DURING THE 1960S

1960, Gastone Nencini (Ita)
1961, Jacques Anquetil (Fra)
1962, Anquetil
1963, Anquetil
1964, Anquetil
1965, Felice Gimondi (Ita)
1966, Lucien Aimar (Fra)
1967, Roger Pingeon (Fra)
1968, Jan Janssen (Ned)
1969, Eddy Merckx (Bel)

▼ 1960s Bianchi.

1970s

Was this the golden era for hand-crafted steel and alloy components? Quite possibly, as the racing machines in the Tour de France during the 1970s were little different from bikes of the previous two decades, so frame and component manufacturers concentrated on the details and aesthetics of parts which were by now hard to improve. For much of the decade, the incremental advances were concentrated on making the bike lighter. Towards the end of the 1970s, aerodynamics began to influence the design of frames and components.

Technical advances were limited. Gears went up to 12, or 10 without cross-chaining, as an extra sprocket was added to the freewheel to make them six-speed. Saddles with moulded plastic bases began to replace the all-leather versions and were

lighter and waterproof. Some had a thin leather-coated padding while others were plain plastic. Titanium parts also began to appear on bikes, from lightweight bolts to frames, the latter seen for the first time under Luis Ocana on his winning ride at the 1973 Tour.

Frames were lighter thanks to new 'extra light' tubesets from British manufacturer Reynolds and Italy's Columbus. Most were still made in the traditional way with tubes inserted into lugs and brazed together using brass or silver. Reynolds 753 tubing was introduced in the mid 1970s and used by the Raleigh team in the 1976 Tour de France. A heat-treated version of the famous 531 tubing, 753 was widely used for pro team frames from then on. Reynolds 531 was launched in 1935 and was for many years the tube of choice for high quality framesets. The overall weight of a racing machine in the

▲ **Quill pedals with toe clips and straps.**

▼ **1970s Bianchi.**

Tour remained at around 9kg (20lb) and getting even a pound or two off the lightest bikes taxed the materials and ingenuity of frame manufacturers and bike builders. The prospect of a complete bike weighing anywhere near the 6.8kg (15lb) lower weight limit of today's Tour bikes would have been considered fantastic at the time. Attempts to build ultra-lightweight machines did result in some impressive weight losses but these bikes were so fragile as to be completely impractical for the real world tough conditions of a three-week race like the Tour.

To shave weight from the bike, frame builders selected lugs with decorative but weight saving shapes cut into them and with holes in bottom brackets. Dropouts had tiny holes drilled into them and lighter castings were used for fork crowns and bottom bracket shells. Components made from aluminium alloy were drilled with holes or had slots cut and filed out of them. Chainsets, chainrings and seatposts were drilled, slotted and fluted. When decoratively painted and polished they looked stunning. These processes put decoration above the saving of a few grams here and there and the risk of failure from an over-drilled component ensured that Tour bikes were often the plainer cousins of the works of art ridden by enthusiast cyclists.

Italy still dominated the components fitted to Tour bikes, primarily with Campagnolo Nuovo Record derailleurs and parts. But there was a healthy selection of alternatives in use from French brands Simplex, Stronglight, Mafac, Lyotard and Mavic. French-made Clement tubular

tyres were widely used on Tour bikes in the 1970s. This was also the decade in which Japanese components, rapidly growing thanks to the consumer bicycle boom in the USA, began to appear on pro bikes. Shimano led the way and in 1973 became the first Japanese brand to equip a team at the Tour de France. Belgian squad Flandria rode on the new Shimano Dura-Ace groupset, winning a stage and beginning an association with professional cycling and the Tour which has resulted in them being the dominant supplier of groupsets to modern pro teams.

By the end of the decade bike designers began to look for other ways to increase the performance of racing bikes. None other than Bernard Hinault rode an aerodynamic bike on some of the time trial stages at the 1979 Tour, winning all four TT stages en route to the second of five Tour victories. His Gitane TT bike had oval-shaped tubes with a small aerofoil behind the head tube. The brake cables were routed along the bars under the bar tape. These innovations got the aero ball rolling and in the following decade time trial bikes experimented further with aero parts and frame designs.

▲ Iconic Campagnolo sidepull brake.

TOUR WINNERS DURING THE 1970S

1970, Eddy Merckx (Bel)
1971, Merckx
1972, Merckx
1973, Luis Ocana (Esp)
1974, Merckx
1975, Bernard Thevenet (Fra)
1976, Lucien Van Impe (Bel)
1977, Thevenet
1978, Bernard Hinault (Fra)
1979, Hinault

1980s

▲ **Early Campagnolo aero caliper brake.**

In the 30 years from the 1950s to the 1980s, the racing bike evolved slowly with only minor changes to its looks and performance. The conservative world of professional cycling has always been cautious in its adoption of new tech but all that changed as the 1980s progressed. Frame materials were dominated by steel but lighter aluminium framesets began to rival steel and by the end of the decade carbon fibre made its first appearance at the Tour. The 1980s also sounded the last post for the traditional pedal with toe clips and straps, as ski-type clip-in pedals made the traditional pedal obsolete. Aerodynamics, which had begun to influence bike design at the end of the 1970s, was recognised increasingly as essential for cycling against the clock and by the end of the decade would determine the result of one of the most exciting Tours in history.

Bikes ridden on road stages in the Tour continued to use mainly hand built steel frames and, apart from incremental improvements in the quality of tubesets, looked and performed little differently from frames of the previous decade. In the 1970s aluminium tubes were seen on frames made by the Italian manufacturer ALAN and Vitus in France and in the 1980s the Vitus Duralinox frame was ridden by several teams in the Tour de France. Using polished lugs, into which the tubes were inserted and bonded, these frames were not much lighter than steel nor as forgiving, but they were stiff and looked more modern than their traditional steel

counterparts. This method of joining tubes gave frame makers their first successful attempts at using basic carbon fibre tubes for cycling and in 1986 French frame builder Look supplied carbon-kevlar framed machines on which Greg LeMond rode in that year's Tour-winning ride. Steel continued to be popular in the peloton throughout the 1980s and it would be another ten years before carbon fibre frames finally took over as the sole frame material of choice for professional riders.

In 1985, French legend Bernard Hinault won his fifth and final Tour de France using a revolutionary white pedal. The distinctive Look pedal had been launched the year before and was based on a ski binding design with a spring-loaded locking and release system. Pedals which locked the shoe to the pedal and did not use toe clips and straps had been tried before but the Look system was the first design which did not require the rider to manually lock and release the shoe. All the cyclist had to do was locate a plastic shoe plate in the tongue of the pedal and push down, clicking it home under a spring-loaded back plate. To release, the rider simply turned out his heel to unclip from the pedal. Look took the peloton by storm and rival 'clipless' systems such as Time, and later Speedplay and Shimano, resulted in the traditional pedal's toe clips and straps becoming almost totally obsolete by 1990.

Aerodynamics took on a far greater significance in the 1980s, with Tour riders influenced by developments in track racing which included low profile frames with cut down upside down handlebars and disc rear wheels. Low profile frames reduced

the frontal area of the machine by a very small amount and the riding position was not significantly different to a rider on the bottom of drop handlebars. A disc wheel on the back reduced turbulence compared to a traditional spoked wheel. These advances were only considered worthwhile on specialist time trial bikes and it would be another 30 years before aerodynamics began to influence the design of road bikes in the Tour. In the 1980s, the only widespread aero trend on road bikes was the adoption of concealed brake cables.

But without question, the most shocking technical moment of the 1980s occurred at the 1989 Tour de France when Greg LeMond used a pair of narrow clip-on triathlon bars and aero helmet to beat Laurent Fignon in the final time trial on the Champs Elysees, winning the race by an incredible eight seconds. In that moment the world of pro cycling woke up to the potential of innovation and as the decade ended, cycling looked ahead with confidence to a future of innovation and change.

TOUR WINNERS DURING THE 1980S
1980, Joop Zoetemelk (Ned)
1981, Bernard Hinault (Fra)
1982, Hinault
1983, Laurent Fignon (Fra)
1984, Fignon
1985, Hinault
1986, Greg LeMond (USA)
1987, Stephen Roche (Irl)
1988, Pedro Delgado (Esp)
1989, LeMond

▲ British Reynolds tubing sticker.

▼ 1980s Raleigh.

There's a pleasing aesthetic to a traditional Campagnolo toolkit.

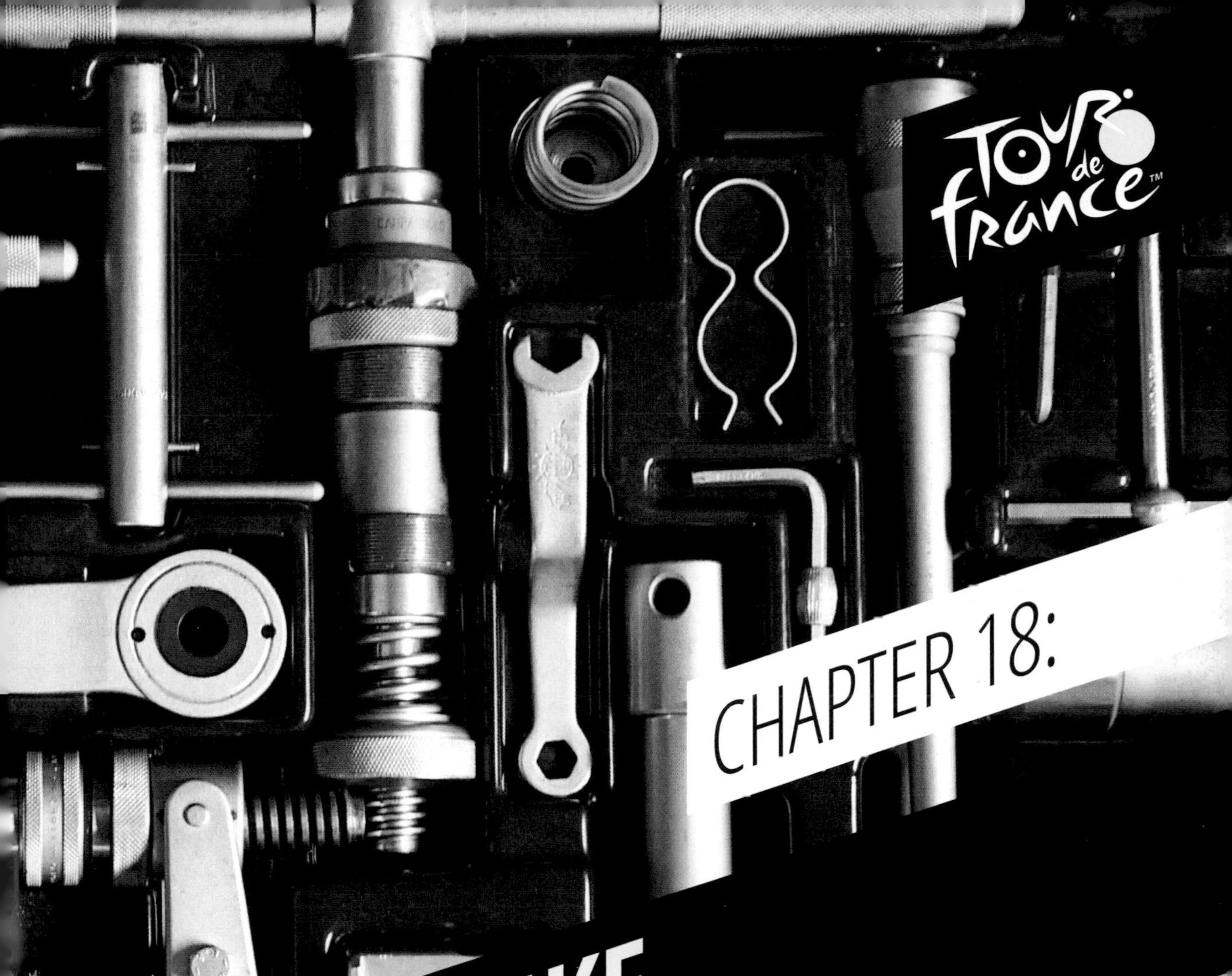

CHAPTER 18:

CLASSIC BIKE MAINTENANCE

The modern Tour de France bike is a very different machine to bikes from the pre-millennium eras. From the late 1980s until the present day, top-end bikes evolved at a pace unmatched since the invention of the safety bike 100 years before. If you are lucky enough to own an original or restored machine from the 1950s onwards, the basics of checking and adjusting key components will ensure it performs as intended.

From the 1950s through to the end of the 1980s, racing bike drivetrains or transmissions changed little and would, outwardly at least, be familiar to riders of the latest machines. The method of transmitting power to the back wheel is the same, with a series of exposed sprockets on a freewheel on the back wheel driven by a chain powered by a chainset fixed to a bottom bracket. Gears are changed manually by cable-operated derailleurs at the freewheel. Where an older bike's transmission departs most obviously from new machines is in the number of sprockets on the freewheel compared to a modern cassette and in the manual component of changing gears.

This is the most significant difference between transmissions pre and post 1990, as that was the year when Shimano introduced the first STI combined brake and gear levers which we take for granted today. Campagnolo followed suit in the 1990s and the traditional method of changing gears using a small lever attached to a boss on the down tube, became obsolete in short order.

Index gearing, which took the deftness out of changing gear manually and replaced it with a lever which clicked into place on every shift, heralded the start of change in 1984. But it was mountain bike 'Rapidfire' technology that revolutionised gear changing and thanks to the clear performance advantage to changing gear with both hands on the bars, pro teams quickly adopted the new combined levers.

The other visual difference with an older bike is the amount of sprockets on the rear wheel. If it's a race bike from the late 1950s through to the 1970s it will have either five or six sprockets. In the 1980s seven-speed freewheels were introduced and although eight-speeds arrived in the 1990s, the width of the extra sprockets put too much stress on the axle and traditional freewheels were phased out in favour of the cassette hub.

Assuming the transmission components are clean and in useable condition there are numerous checks and adjustments which can be made to optimise their performance. There are no automatic elements to any part on the traditional drivetrain. Once the gears have been checked for alignment and their limits of throw, there is no indexing function to fine tune as there would be on a modern rear derailleur. With a manual gear shift the key to maintaining its smooth function is to keep the components clean, lubricated and free from excessive slack or wear.

▲ Inspecting an Eroica bike.

▶ Traditional components are simple to work on.

TOUR TIP

As with any classic machine, it saves a lot of time and expense if you can start with an example in good overall condition, which just needs a full service to get it back on the road for an Eroica event.

DRIVETRAIN CHECKS

▲ Classic bikes await their riders before an Eroica ride.

1 Before making any significant adjustments to the rear derailleur, first check the alignment of the gear itself on the dropout hanger. Remove the rear derailleur using a hex key on the recessed bolt which secures it to the dropout hanger. Carefully screw in the alignment tool and, with a precision ruler, measure the distance from the rim to the handle of the alignment tool at various points around the wheel. Double check the wheel itself is true. If there is more than a 3mm difference the hanger may need to be very carefully tweaked, using the handle of the tool.

2 Set the top limit screw on the rear derailleur. With the derailleur screwed back in and with the chain on the small ring at the front, carefully go up through the gears until the chain is sitting on the biggest sprocket nearest the spokes. The gear should be quiet and running smoothly. Get behind the derailleur and check that the sprocket and both jockey wheels are perfectly aligned. Using a screwdriver on the top limit screw, screw it carefully in until the derailleur just starts to move away from the spokes. Back it off to where it was before and pull back the gear lever to ensure the derailleur is a few millimetres away from the spokes.

3 Set limiters on the front derailleur. Like the rear derailleur, two screws control the throw of the mechanism and on the front these are designed to prevent the chain being thrown off the big and small chainrings. Put the gears into the big ring and smallest sprocket and the small ring and biggest sprocket and visually check that the chain is not rubbing the front derailleur cage. It only needs to just clear the inside of the cage on the small ring and the outside on the big ring and that is where the limit screw should be set.

4 Down tube gear levers are secured with screws which can be tightened via a D-ring through the head of the screw or by a screwdriver. The lever is under constant tension from the springs in the front and rear derailleurs. The lever should be assembled without oil or grease and tightened so that it moves smoothly in use, but is tight enough to resist the pull from the gear mechanisms.

5 Check the alignment of the front derailleur. To do this properly it is best to loosen the bolt that secures the operating cable to the derailleur. Loosen the bolt that secures the derailleur to the brazed-on gear bracket. If the derailleur is secured with a band around the seat tube, slacken off the bolt on the clamp until the derailleur can be moved without sliding down. Position the bottom edge of the outer cage plate 1–3mm above the teeth on the big ring. Align the cage so that it sits parallel to the chain through its arc.

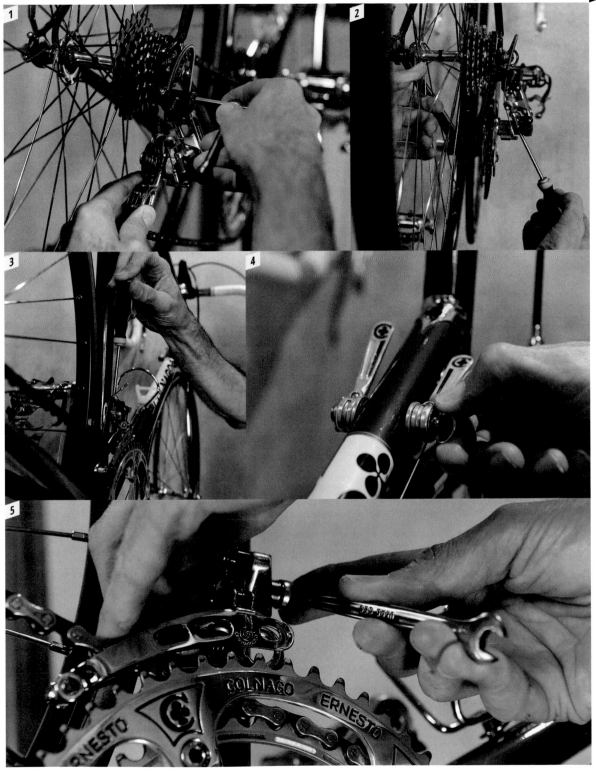

6 Check the pinch bolts on the front and rear derailleurs. Push both levers as far forward as they go, until they reach their stops. Check the cables for any excess slack – they should be tight enough to move after the smallest movement at the lever. To tighten the cables, undo the pinch bolt and with flat-nose pliers on the exposed cable pull it tight and do up the pinch bolt. On old rear derailleurs there is no micro adjust so this is the only way to adjust the cable.

7 Check the chain length. This is to determine if the chain is the correct length, neither too long nor short which can both lead to drivetrain inefficiency and wear. To check if the chain is long enough put it on the big ring and engage the second biggest sprocket on the freewheel. The rear derailleur jockey arm should be almost but not fully extended, with the bottom jockey wheel slightly ahead of the one above.

8 To check the chain is not too long put it on the small ring and the second smallest sprocket. The jockey arm will be tucked in under the derailleur body but the upper jockey wheel should not be touching the sprocket and there should be a clear and quiet run of the chain through the jockey wheels. The derailleur should have just enough spring travel to maintain tension in the lower run of the chain.

9 Check the chainrings and sprockets. When the teeth and valleys of these components are worn the teeth lose their flat tops and can become pointed. In the valleys in between each tooth the uniform semi-circle resembles an uneven wave if the chainring is worn. On the freewheel sprockets the most frequently used ones in the centre of the block are likely to show the most wear.

10 Under the bottom bracket, check the condition of the cables and guides. On steel bottom bracket shells the cables are exposed to a lot of water and grime thrown back by the front wheel. To prolong the life of the cables and encourage smooth running, slide short lengths of modern cable inner housing along them. Tension from the cables should hold the inners in place. If not, a small dab of superglue will fix them in the bottom bracket guides.

TOUR TIP If the sprockets and chainrings are in good condition, a new chain can be fitted but make sure it is the correct size for the number of sprockets on the rear wheel.

OTHER DIFFERENCES

▲ Check alloy bars are straight and undamaged.

▼ Traditional dropouts allow the wheel a small amount of fore-aft adjustment.

Steel racing bikes from the pre-1990s differ from a modern carbon fibre machine in numerous areas. The rear dropouts on a steel frame are not vertical like a modern bike but look like an elongated C into which the wheel is inserted. There is no adjustment on a vertical dropout, the wheel is simply pulled up into it and locked in with the quick-release. Traditional steel frames had adjustable dropouts which allowed precise location of the rear wheel and could be used to ensure the wheel was straight even if the back end was not precisely aligned. They come in long and short lengths with both types incorporating a threaded gear hanger for the rear derailleur.

A traditional dropout with gear hanger cannot be replaced like a modern gear hanger and care must be taken not to bend it as it can only be bent back into line. If that is not possible the frame will have to go to a frame builder who will remove it, braze in a new one and re-spray the frame. Rear dropout screws, if fitted, make putting in the back wheel much easier once they are adjusted to the desired position. As on all older machines these components as well as the quick-release skewers should be carefully checked for corrosion and kept lubricated.

Handlebars will normally be alloy and should always be examined for any signs of cracks, bends or crash damage. If in doubt change them for modern versions in retro styles or new old stock bars. Anatomical bars and short-drop designs did not exist pre-1990s so be prepared for a longer reach to the drops on most styles. Also make sure you are happy with the position of the brake levers before fitting new cables as it is important not to have them too long or short above the bars.

Adjusting caliper brakes is not dissimilar to working on modern side-pull calipers. As with any cable-operated system the condition of the cables determines how smoothly they operate and on an older machine it is well worth changing unlined brake cables for modern lined ones which are much smoother and do not require lubrication.

Even more alien to new cyclists are the pedal systems used by their forebears. Toe clips and straps are obligatory in many Eroica events. Original parts are often in poor condition but reproduction toe clips and straps are worth considering. Toe clips and straps should be used with traditional shoes with a slotted shoe plate either nailed or bolted in place. Modern reproduction shoes with shoe plates bolted on are well worth considering over a used pair.

CLASSIC BIKE MAINTENANCE
BEARINGS

It is rare to find a traditional threaded headset on a modern bike. Threaded headsets are significantly different to the now universal Aheadset style threadless headsets. Threaded headsets and stems are not complicated but they do require specific cycling spanners to perform adjustments. A modern threadless headset is much better at staying in adjustment and withstanding the demands put upon it. It does, however, require a decision as to the length of the steerer and a series of spacers below and sometimes above the stem, to set the correct handlebar height. A threaded steerer is separate to the stem, which sits inside the steerer and can be easily adjusted up or down and tightened with a single hex key.

Traditional bottom brackets, the bearing and axle on which the crank and chainset turn, are also quite unlike modern oversized bottom brackets with sealed bearings often located outside the bracket shell. How the cranks are attached to the axle is also different, with traditional axles usually employing a square taper onto which the cranks are tightened. The bearings are loose and not sealed, they need to be packed with grease, checked regularly and adjusted if there is any movement in the axle. Headsets and bottom brackets require considerably more care and attention than their modern counterparts but if you start with quality versions which are greased

and in good condition there is no reason why they should not last a long time with periodic maintenance.

Cup and cone bearings are still in use on modern wheels and on older versions they can run as smoothly and reliably as any wheel bearing. Again, like the other main bearings on older bikes if the condition of the hubs is good, they are greased and adjusted correctly, the wheels can be used for at least a year before checking for any play in the bearings. To adjust cup and cone bearings you will need a pair of flat-cone spanners, which also fit the flats on a caliper brake.

Determining if there is play in a cup and cone bearing is a finicky process and best done using a vice in which the wheel can be clamped. These are small bearings and it can take several goes juggling the lock nut and the cone with both spanners before no play is evident in the axle. At the precise point at which there is no play the bearing will run smoothly.

▼ Traditional headset exploded view.

BEARINGS CHECKS

1 Traditional headsets work loose over time and should be checked regularly. Stand beside the bike and hold the bars on the drops. Apply the front brake and gently rock the bars back and forth. A slight clunk and a tiny amount of slack in the headset will be evident if the headset is loose. To check if there is pitting in the bearings, lift the front wheel just off the ground and with one hand slowly turn the bars. If it feels notchy or rough the bearing may need servicing or replacement. There can often be a notch in the straight-ahead position which can affect the handling of the bike.

2 The lock nut and upper bearing cup can only be adjusted using specialist cycling tools which are designed to be used in close proximity on the headset stack. As a result they have to be thin enough to sit one above the other while also long enough to exert enough loading to prevent the headset coming loose. Italian Campagnolo headset tools will fit other brands of headset and are dual purpose, with 32mm (1¼in) hexagonal flats for the headset on one side and the pins and C-shaped peg wrench at the other for bottom bracket adjustment.

3 The threaded headset is simple to adjust and consists of an upper bearing cup and lock nut located on the threaded steerer column of the fork which is inserted in the frame head tube. Both the upper bearing cup and the lock nut have hexagonal flats on them and are engineered to be as flat as possible to keep the stack height low so that the stem can go as low as possible. It is easy for the tools to slip off the cup, and especially the lock nut, so take extra care when the tools are positioned on the flats of each component.

4 To adjust the headset, first undo the lock nut – the top nut in the stack. Just take the tension out of the nut, it is not necessary to unscrew it until it is loose. With the tool on the flats of the upper bearing cup, make a 1/6 turn, no more, and rock the bike back and forth, feeling for any clunks or movement. Continue to screw down the upper bearing using the small turns and rocking the front end. When there is no movement left, lift the front wheel and check the bearing is not too tight. It should feel smooth while turning the bars, which should just flop from side to side when the hands are removed. Holding the tool locked with your left hand on the upper bearing, place the other tool on the lock nut so that the tool resembles an 'A'. Tighten the lock nut onto the upper bearing, taking care not to let it turn under the lock nut. Double-check the adjustment as it can take a few goes to get the headset spot on.

5 Check the bottom bracket. Remove the chain, and rest it carefully over the bottom bracket shell where it is not touching the chainrings. Hold the cranks in both hands and rock them alternately as if you are trying to turn the bike on its axis. Feel for any movement or clunking noises.

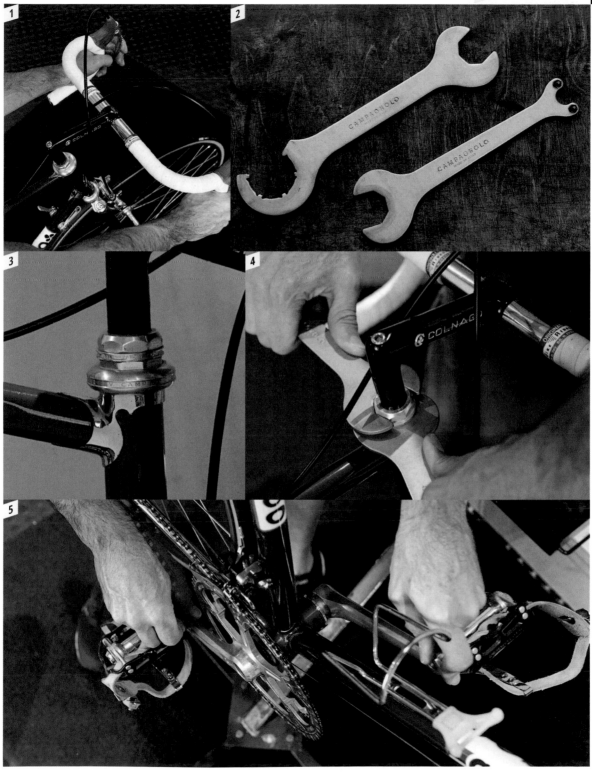

There should be none at all, as even the smallest amount of movement indicates that the bearings are out of adjustment. At the same time turn the pedals in the normal way and feel for any roughness.

6 Remove the bolts and washers from the cranks. A socket tool will not fit inside the crank, you need a crank spanner which is designed to slip over the nut in the threaded hole of the crank. If it is fitted, first remove the dust cap which screws into the hole. They often have two pinholes and can be removed with sharp-nose pliers. With the crank bolt exposed, position the tool snugly over it and undo the bolt. Make sure you remove the washer. It should not be overtight as that may indicate excess wear to the square-tapered hole in the crank.

7 Take the extractor tool out and back off the threaded plunger nut. Make sure it is screwed out almost to the limits of its thread. Make sure the threads of the crank are clean, a little machine oil will help the extractor go in. Taking care not to cross-thread it, screw in the extractor fully, until it goes no further and just starts to bind. Screw in the plunger bolt by hand until it makes contact with the end of the bottom bracket axle. Using the same crank tool as before, tighten the plunger. It will bind and feel very tight but keep turning until the crank begins to release itself from the taper on the bottom bracket axle. At this point another half turn or so will remove the entire crank from the axle.

8 To adjust the bottom bracket it's worth leaving the right-hand side crank and chainset on to check for play. On the left-hand side, undo the toothed lock ring using the other end of the headset tool. It does not have to come off, just enough to reveal a thread or two. Using the peg wrench, tighten the bearing cup no more than a 1/8 turn. Use the crank on the other side to feel for play but be careful not to overtighten the bearing. Hold the bearing with the peg wrench and do up the lock ring, making sure it has located securely on all the teeth of the ring.

9 To check the wheel bearings, first remove the wheel from the bike and unscrew the quick-release skewer, taking care not to lose the springs. Note the way the cone-shaped springs go, with the widest part away from the bike.

10 Ideally, put the wheel in an axle vice as that is the best way to feel for any movement in the bearings by rocking the rim from side to side. You need flat-cone spanners to adjust the bearings. Undo the lock ring with one spanner and seat the cone bearing 1/8 turn with the other while checking for movement in the rim. As soon as there is no movement at the rim, the bearing is correctly adjusted but be careful when doing up the lock ring as it can compress the bearing. So can the quick-release if done up tight – try backing off the cone against the lock ring just as it is being tightened.

GENERAL CHECKS

▲ Fitting a back wheel on a traditional bike.

1 Horizontal rear dropouts allow the wheel to move back and forth in the slots of the dropout. With the wheel in the dropouts there should be about 20mm (¾in) of adjustment. With the wheel at the back of the dropouts the wheelbase is at its longest and there will be clearance for a fatter tyre in between the chainstays behind the bottom bracket. If the biggest sprocket is a 28 or more it may be necessary to adjust the rear wheel to ensure the top jockey wheel clears the sprocket.

2 Quick-release skewers. On old bikes unscrew the quick-release skewers and slide them out of the hollow wheel axles. As you do so hold the left-hand acorn adjuster nut and take care to also hold onto the conical spring on that side. Withdraw the skewer from the lever side, again taking care not to lose the spring. Clean and apply oil to the lever joint, cam and threads of the skewer. Replace the skewer in the hub axle opposite the freewheel and on the right side of the front wheel, note that the widest part of the conical springs should face the lever and nut faces.

3 Put the wheel back in the frame dropouts. With hands on the lever and nut, turn the lever and micro adjust the nut until the lever closes firmly. Some pro mechanics put their fingers around the spokes to pull on the lever but on old wheels it is safer to pull on the frame or fork. Push the lever with the palm of your hand. If it leaves an imprint in your hand that is usually tight enough. Note the position of the levers for ease of use. If it's too close to the frame or fork it can be hard to undo.

4 Check and adjust rear dropout screws. Make sure they are clean and pre-oiled with spray or light oil before attempting to screw them in or out. Put the back wheel with the quick-release undone into the dropouts with the axle positioned as far forward as it will go while still in contact with the dropout. Ensure that the tyre is positioned centrally between the chainstays near the bottom bracket and that there is at least 5mm clearance each side. Do up the quick-release and then screw in the dropout screws until they meet the axle of the wheel and can go no further.

5 Handlebar angle and cables. Older handlebars often have deeper, more rounded shaped drops and should be set up with the bottom section of the bar either parallel to the ground or pointing slightly down. A good rule of thumb is to align the end of the bar, where the bar end sits, parallel with the angle of the head tube. Exposed brake cables should have a natural loop from both levers. They should be long enough to allow the bars to turn freely from lock to lock.

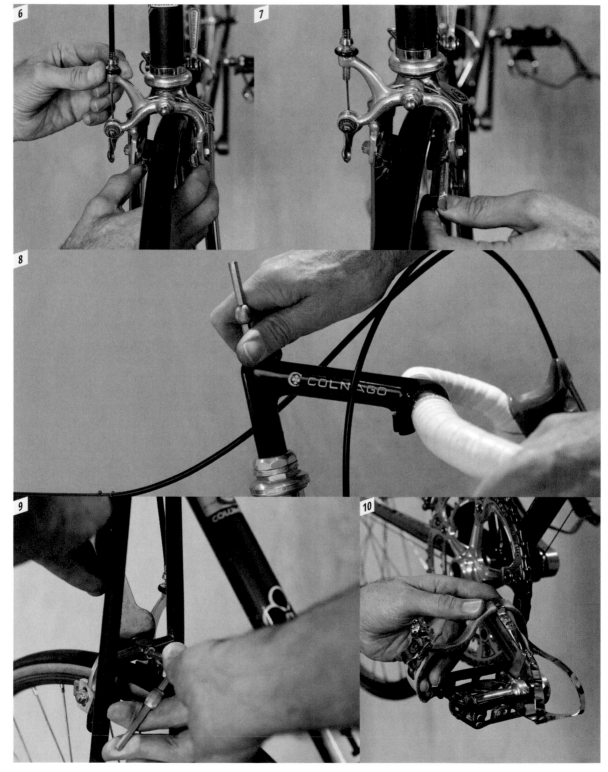

6 Adjust brakes. Similar to a modern caliper side-pull brake, the older models are adjusted by setting the cable in the pinch bolt and then fine tuning with the threaded barrel adjuster. Screw the barrel adjuster fully home so that the threads are showing below the caliper arm. With the pads pulled onto the rim by hand, undo the pinch bolt and allow the cable to find its place, then do up the bolt. When replacing brake cables use modern lined inner and outer cables as they are much smoother, do not need greasing and look the same as older unlined versions.

7 Replacing brake pads. Wear marks on older brake pads perform the same function as current versions. When the pads are worn below the marks the pads should be changed. Original pads may be hard to source and the pad compound not as effective as a modern version. If you want to keep the triangular wheel guides which sit below the pads you may have to use the original cartridge with new old stock pads inserted.

8 Stem bolt. The stem bolt is recessed in the top of the stem and has a 6mm hex head. It is a long bolt with an expander cone which clamps the stem to the head tube. Unlike a modern threadless headset, this bolt does not act on the headset bearings but has the duel function of adjusting and clamping the stem. Before adjusting the stem put some light oil around the bottom of the stem where it enters the head tube and allow it to soak

overnight. To adjust the stem up and down and side to side undo the bolt just until you can feel it unload on the expander cone. Carefully turn the bars with the front wheel between your legs until the stem moves. Shuffle the stem up or down, being careful not to exceed the limits marked on the side. Align the stem by eye in-line with the top tube. Tighten the bolt, not overtight but tighter than a threadless top nut.

9 Adjust the brakes with cone spanners. If one side of the caliper side-pull brake is too close to the rim the brake can be adjusted with a cone spanner and hex key. A slim cone spanner is inserted behind the caliper arms and engages with flats on a spacer. With a hex key, usually 5mm, inserted in the brake, slightly undo the brake bolt. Use the cone spanner to rotate the caliper arms until the brake pads sit equidistant on the rim and do up the brake bolt while holding the cone spanner in position.

10 Toe clips and straps. Make sure you have the correct size toe clips, which should be marked from S to XL. Check the two nuts and bolts clamping the clips to the pedal are in good condition and not loose. Check the toe straps are in good condition. When threading them through the slots on either side of the pedal body, put a twist in the straps to prevent them pulling through when they are tightened onto the shoe. A plastic tab on the end of the strap, secured with a grub screw, makes it easier to do up the strap after pulling away.

LE TOUR
AND BEYOND

In this book, I hope you have got a flavour of the life of the professional cycling mechanic, as well as picked up some of their good habits and handy tips. Everyone involved in the Tour de France — there is a cast of thousands in one of the world's biggest annual sporting event — has got a job to do and the mechanics are very much part of the show.

After the cyclists, all 176 of them, the four or so mechanics on each of the 22 teams are responsible for maintaining all their bikes as well as attending to their needs from team cars on every stage of the race.

They will be seen during the live TV feed of each stage whenever a rider punctures or crashes and the camera will also follow riders back to team cars where mechanics supply them with drinks and cooling bags, and hang precariously from the open window to make adjustments to bike and rider as the race speeds onwards.

At stage starts and finishes crowds surge around team buses where, once again, the mechanics are watched intently as they make final checks and tweaks to the eight team bikes before the stage, and pack away the dusty machines after a day's racing.

Back at the team hotel, where they might expect to escape the clamour, more fans gather to watch them go through their daily routines of washing, checking and repairing.

▶ Mechanic and rider are the team within a team.

For those three weeks in July, the mechanics put in a tremendous amount of work, outside in all conditions and often under the scrutiny of others. Glamourous it is not, although many of them enjoy interacting with the public and actually revel in the high pressure environment of the Tour.

There are many excellent bicycle mechanics doing a brilliant job in shops and sheds but only a few have the desire or temperament to throw themselves into life on the road with a pro team.

SKILLS TRANSFER

You may not want to be a mechanic on a Tour de France team but that does not mean you cannot be as good at maintaining your bike and, in some respects, even better as the heavy workload of a pro can rule out the finishing touches of a perfectionist. That said the Tour mechanics love to show their skills off on one-off machines like the ones ridden by the classification leaders.

For the home mechanic the practical pages in this book emphasise the importance of keeping your bike and transmission as clean as it was when new, and of making regular checks on components. This will ensure fastenings are not coming loose, components are damaged and that gears and brakes, are in perfect adjustment. It will also flag up if consumables like chains and brake pads are due for replacement.

As important as daily component checks are the condition of your tyres, which should be inspected before every ride for excessive wear or damage. Riders

and mechanics share a keen interest in tyre types, their condition and running pressures. It explains in part why pro cyclists continue to favour tubular tyres, which require laborious preparation and fitment with a tacky glue. Their performance advantages are marginal but in pro racing every fraction of an advantage counts.

Regular cyclists opted long ago for much easier to fit tyre choices but that should not affect how important it is to treat your tyres with the same reverence as a pro mechanic treats his beloved tubulars.

ENJOY IT!

They may look serious and under pressure but take a Tour mechanic to one side and ask him if he enjoys his job and all of them without exception will say, no, they don't like their job, they love it! You cannot work for three weeks 24/7 on multiple bikes every day without being totally committed and devoted to your craft.

If you can take some of the pride and diligence displayed by the pro mechanics in this book, and use it on your own machines you will not only have a safer, faster, better looking bike, you will gain another skill to enrich your enjoyment of cycling, the king of sports.

▲ A fitting place to finish: the pack riding on the Champs Elysees in 2018.

GLOSSARY

A

Aero Any component or item designed to reduce drag or place the rider in a more aerodynamic position

Aero bars Commonly used for time trial bar extensions that place the rider in an aero position with elbows and hands close together. Can also be used for conventional drop handlebars with aerofoil top sections

Allen bolt Also known as a hex bolt, is a bolt with recessed hexagonal faces which can only be turned with an Allen or hex key tool

B

Bearing Used to reduce friction between moving parts, often as a sealed annular ball bearing race in bikes

Block Traditional arrangement of sprockets on rear hub, pre-cassette, that contains the freewheel and is screwed in place

Bottom bracket Bearing on which the chainset and cranks turn, fitted to the bottom bracket shell of the frame

Bunch Main group of riders, also known as the pack or peloton

C

Cadence Pedalling speed measured in revolutions on one crank, per minute

Cassette Modern arrangement of sprockets that slide onto a freehub body and are secured with a lock-ring

Chainring Large sprocket or ring with teeth screwed to the chainset spider. Usually two but can be a single ring or triple

Chainstay Horizontal tubes from the bottom bracket to the rear dropouts

Classic Famous and historic one-day professional bike race

Classification Competition within the Tour, which could be for the best sprinter, climber, young rider or team

Cleat Shoe plate attached to the bottom of a racing shoe that engages with the pedal

Clincher Most popular and conventional tyre for enthusiast riders, clincher or wired-on tyres are 'open' and fixed to the rim with a wire or composite bead

Clipless Modern quick-release type pedal that does not feature traditional toe-clips

Commissaire Race judge or official in a car or on the back of a motorbike

Crank Arms onto which the pedals are attached on both sides of the bottom bracket

Crank spider Right hand crank with four or five small extensions into which the chainrings are screwed

D

Derailleur Front and rear gear mechanisms that literally derail the chain from one sprocket to another

Directeur Sportif Sports director on a team, often driving the number one and two team cars behind the bunch

Disc brake Braking system using a metal rotor or disc attached to the wheel hub and operated by a caliper fixed to the fork end or rear stay

Down tube Diagonal tube which runs from the head tube to the bottom bracket shell

Drafting Riding in the slipstream of another rider or vehicle

Drivetrain All the mechanical components used to drive the rear wheel

Drop-out Slot or threaded hole into which the front and rear wheels are attached

Drops The curved part of drop handlebars. 'On the drops' is riding with hands on the drops

E

Elastomer Compressible damping material used to soak up vibration

Expander bolt Cone shaped bolt that tightens against the inside of a tube as it is turned

F

Ferrule Cap on end of cable that allows it to sit snugly against a cable stop

Frameset Frame including the fork

Freehub Hub with integral freewheel and body for gear cassette

Freewheel Mechanism with sprung pawls that lock the cassette or gear cluster when pedalling and allow it to turn when not

G

General Classification (GC) Also known as overall classification (OC), is the way the Tour riders are ranked at the end of each stage based on their overall elapsed time from all the previous stages

Green jersey Worn by the leader of the points classification, contested by the best sprinters

Groupset Assembly of parts from one manufacture, usually enough to complete the drivetrain and braking

Grub screw Headless screw often used to adjust derailleur gears

H

Headset Bearings at top and bottom of head tube that hold the fork and allow it to turn. Threadless and threaded type

Head tube Short tube at the front of the frame to which the top and down tubes are attached

Hydraulic Sealed system for braking using fluid

I

Individual time trial Timed race for solo rider over a set distance or course

J

Jersey Cycling top, long or short sleeved usually with pockets on the back

Jig Device for measuring, setting up and working on bikes, shoes and wheels

King of the Mountains (KOM) Leader of the best climber's competition, based on points scored at the summits of each classified climb

L

Lock ring or nut Nut that tightens onto a bearing cup or similar, holding it firmly in place.

Maillot jaune French for yellow jersey, symbol of the leader of the Tour

Mechanism Another word for the derailleur, also known as a mech

Musette Flat cotton bag with strap filled with energy food handed up to riders at feed zones and from team cars during the stage

N

Neutral Neutral support is the Mavic service team and neutral zone are kilometres after the stage start which are not raced until the pack reaches the 'zero kilometres' start banner

Nipple Barrel or pear-shaped end of cable, which fits into brake or gear lever

O

Orthotics Custom insoles for racing shoes

P

Play Slight movement between two parts

Polka-dot jersey White jersey with red spots worn by the leader of the mountains' classification, contested by the leading climbers

Prime Intermediate sprint during the stage with points counting towards the sprinters' classification green jersey

Prologue Short time trial at the very start of the Tour

Q

Q-factor Width measurement between feet on the pedals

Quick-release Lever on a cam attached to threaded rod and dome nut that releases when the lever opens

R

Radial Spoking pattern in which the spokes are laced in a star pattern without crossing

Rainbow jersey White top with rainbow bands worn by world champion

Road race Race between two points along roads contested by a bunch of riders

Rollers Type of static trainer most commonly used for warming up for track events

S

Seat post Pillar that fits into the seat tube and onto which is bolted the saddle

Seat stay Thin frame tube extending diagonally from the top of the seat tube to the rear dropouts

Seat tube Frame tube between the bottom bracket and saddle clamp
Service course Team headquarters, store and service centre

Shifter Lever or paddle used to change gears

Sidewall Sides of a tyre

Spindle Type of axle

Sprocket Thin cog denoted by numbers of teeth that makes up a cassette or block

Stage One of 20 or 21 individual days' of racing of the Tour de France

Steerer tube Part of the fork that sits inside the frame head tube

Stem Piece that holds the handlebars and is clamped to the fork steerer

T

Tapered A tube or bar with a decreasing diameter along its length

Team A professional cycling team may have up to 30 riders but only eight are selected for the Tour

Team time trial Timed race by the whole team over a set course

Threadless Modern headset style that does not need a tradition fork steerer with threaded top

Time trial Timed race for individual riders over a set course

Top tube Frame tube that connects the top of the seat tube with the top of the head tube

Tops Straight part of handlebar – riding 'on the tops'

Transmission The chain, gears, chainset and sprockets that drive the back wheel

Truing Process of adjusting a wheel until it runs 'true'

Tubular tyre Lightweight racing tyre that is sewn together and glued to the wheel rim

Turbo Device that holds the back wheel of the bike on a roller and is used for training, warming up and down

U

UCI Union Cycliste Internationale, the cycling world governing body

V

Velodrome French for cycling track

Vertical dropouts Modern type of dropout into which the wheel is easily slotted

W

Watt Unit of power measured by power meters on cranks and displayed on head unit on bars

Workstand Portable support that holds the bike up for ease of maintenance and washing

Y

Yellow jersey Yellow top worn by the leader of the General Classification of the Tour de France

Z

Zone Piece of road or area most commonly for feeding riders or neutralised at the start of the stage

INDEX

CREDITS

The publishers would like to thank the following sources for their kind permission to reproduce the pictures in this book. Key: T=top, B=bottom, L=left, C=centre, R=right.

Alamy: /JWO: 20

Carlton Books: /Andy Jones: 32-33, 35TL, 35TR, 35L, 35R, 36BL, 36R, 36BR, 37TL, 37TR, 38C, 38BL, 38BR, 39T, 39C, 39B, 43T, 43B, 45T, 45BL, 45BR, 46TL, 46B, 47, 48B, 78, 79TL, 79B, 80BL, 99, 101TL, 101TR, 101L 101C, 101R, 101BL, 101BR, 102TL, 102TR, 102C, 105BL, 105BC, 105BR, 106TL, 106TC, 106TR, 106L, 106R, 106BL, 106BR, 107, 110L, 110R, 110BL, 110BR, 111C, 111BL, 111BR, 113BL, 113BR, 114B, 133TL, 133TR, 133L, 133R, 133B, 135TL, 135TR, 135C, 135BL, 135BR, 136T, 136C, 136B, 138, 139T, 139C, 139BL, 139BR, 140BL, 140BR, 141BL, 141BR, 143T, 143L, 143BL, 143BR, 165TL, 165TR, 165R, 166TL, 166B, 169TL, 169TR, 169L, 169R, 169BL, 169BR, 170TL, 170TR, 170L, 170R, 170BL, 170BR, 171, 172-173, 180, 181TR, 181B, 182-183, 185, 187TL, 187TR, 187L, 187R, 187B, 189TL, 189TR, 189L, 189R, 189B, 190B, 191, 193TL, 193TR, 193L, 193R, 193B, 195TL, 195TR, 195L, 195R, 195B, 197T, 197L, 197R, 197BL, 197BR, 198TL, 198TR, 198C, 198BL, 198BR

Christoph Deike: 28TL, 28B, 29, 30T, 30B, 31TL, 31TR

Getty Images: /Marco Bertorello/AFP: 118TL, 128B, 129; /Lionel Bonaventure/AFP: 92; / Gabriel Bouys/AFP: 196; /Giuseppe Cacace/ AFP: 186; /Jean Catuffe: 201; /Luc Claessen: 63; /Tim de Waele: 22-23, 24, 52-53, 55, 66, 67, 69B, 70TL, 70B, 108-109, 114TL, 150BL; / Eric Feferberg/AFP: 134; /Chris Graythen: 12,

15, 72-73, 94R, 110TL, 113TR, 115B, 122-123, 128TL, 148BL, 148BR, 167; /Bryn Lennon: 124, 140TL, 146TL, 158; /Ljubaphoto: 49; /Thomas Lohnes: 184; /Philippe Lopez/AFP: 27BL, 48TL; /Jeff Pachoud/AFP: 27BR, 60-61, 64, 65, 71, 89; /Doug Pensinger: 144-145; /Joel Saget/AFP: 137; /Justin Setterfield: 59, 119, 126, 168; /Javier Soriano/AFP: 118BL; /Kenzo Tribouillard/AFP: 149B, 151; /Kei Tsuji/Tim de Waele/Corbis: 16, 21, 62, 68, 69TR, 75, 112, 149TR, 152-153

Nick Legan: 159BL, 159BC, 159BR, 161TL, 161TR, 161L, 161C, 161R, 161BL, 161BR

Offside Sports Photography: /L'Equipe: 8-9, 103TR; /Presse Sports: 25, 76, 77, 84

Shutterstock: /Ansario: 141TR, 143R; /Laurent Cipriani/AP: 82-83; /Peter Dejong/AP: 162-163; /Yorick Jansens/EPA/REX: 51; /Kim Ludbrook/ EPA/REX: 7, 127

Yuzuru Sunada: 10-11, 13, 14, 18, 34, 40-41, 42, 44, 50, 54, 56, 58, 74, 80TL, 80-81, 96-97, 98TL, 98BR, 103BR, 104, 105TR, 118BR, 121, 125, 130-131, 132, 154, 155, 157, 164, 174TL, 174B, 175, 176, 177, 178TL, 178B, 179, 190TL, 200

Graham Watson: 57, 85, 87TL, 87TR, 87L, 87C, 87R, 87BL 87BR, 88TL, 88TR, 88B, 90, 91, 93TL, 93TR, 93L, 93R, 93B, 94L, 94TL, 94TR, 94B, 115TR, 116-117, 120TL, 120B, 146B, 147, 148TL, 150TL

Every effort has been made to acknowledge correctly and contact the source and/or copyright holder of each picture and Carlton Books Limited apologises for any unintentional errors or omissions that will be corrected in future editions of this book.

Publisher's notes:
The publisher would like to thank the following people for their expert advice and guidance in putting together this book.

A big thank you to Luke Edwardes-Evans for his tireless devotion to building this book. To Andy Jones and Rohan Dubash (www.doctord.co.uk) for their assistance and advice in capturing the finer details of some marvellous machines. To Richard Hemmington at Pinarello UK, plus Team Sky and Geraint Thomas, for the loan of their outstanding bike. And to Yuzuru Sunada for taking the time to capture behind-the-scenes images at the Tour de France.